Cases in Compensation 11.1e

Copyright © 2013 by George T. Milkovich and Barry Gerhart

The authors acknowledge with thanks the contributions of many colleagues to Cases in Compensation, particularly those adopters who, over the years, took the time to e-mail us with their comments or talk with us. We especially wish to thank Robert Amann, Lisa Burke, Kristl Davison, Marilyn Eastman, Allen Engle, Barry Friedman, Cindy Fukami, Ingrid Smithey Fulmer, Barbara Hassell, Sanjay Menon, David Moore, Hesan Ahmed Quazi, Dow Scott, Tom Stone, Ed Tomlinson, Charlie Trevor, and Alix Valenti. A special thanks to Jerry Newman who has been our coauthor on the accompanying textbook Compensation and to Carolyn Milkovich and Heather Gerhart.

cases.in.compensation@gmail.com

ISBN: 978-0-945601-00-5

Table of Contents

Introduction

A main theme in the *Compensation* textbook is that compensation decisions should be aligned with an organization's business strategy, values, and its business environment. You will be the compensation decision maker for FastCat charged with creating this alignment. Currently, FastCat does not have a formal compensation plan. Little systematic thought has been given to employees' salaries. To remedy this situation, FastCat has hired you to bring some order to the way their employees are paid. Combine the information in this manual with the information in your textbook, classroom discussions, and your instructor's directions to arrive at your recommendations.

Exhibit 1
Three Interrelated Phases

Phase I: Internal Alignment: Design an internal job structure based on the work and its relative importance to FastCat objectives. Job evaluation is a key tool.

Phase II: External Competitiveness: Price the structure (i.e, choose a pay level) based on external market forces, competitors' practices, and FastCat's objectives. Pay surveys provide the data.

Phase III: Performance and Management: Decide how and how much to vary pay according to performance; manage the system; control costs; and evaluate your work.

HOW THE PHASES FIT TOGETHER

The case has three interrelated phases that parallel the pay model used in the *Compensation* textbook (**Exhibit 1**). The work you do in each phase will lay the groundwork for the next phase. As you complete the three phases, you will address the same compensation issues that managers face in organizations today.

Begin by reading FastCat's history. Pay attention to its values, the environment it faces, and what its leaders say about its business strategy. Then, establish FastCat's compensation objectives—what you want your compensation system to achieve. Setting objectives is the first part of establishing the compensation strategy.

In *Phase I*, you will examine a sample of FastCat jobs and design a structure based on factors important for FastCat's success. FastCat's history, its business, and what the company leadership says it wants to achieve will provide guidance for those decisions. The policies and programs you choose and how you design them should help FastCat achieve its objectives.

In *Phase II*, you will design a market pay survey data that tells what FastCat's competitors are paying their employees in specific jobs. Next, you will decide which competitors to benchmark FastCat's pay against as an input to your choice of a pay level for FastCat's jobs. You will then use the market pay survey data on pay level from these competitors and apply that information to price (i.e., assign a pay level to) the job structure (based on job evaluation points) you designed in Phase I. The result will be a pay structure. Software written for this case will help in this analysis.

In *Phase III*, you will recommend pay rates for individual FastCat employees within the pay structure. You will explore possibilities for basing pay on their individual performance and/or the company's performance. You will also recommend a policy on benefits. Again, software written for this case will help your analysis. Additionally, you will recommend how to manage your compensation system and evaluate your work in light of the objectives you set for it.

Keep in mind these important questions: How will your system help FastCat achieve its business objectives? Do your decisions from all three phases fit together and complement each other? Or will the effects of some decisions undermine others?

Remember that you are not designing a generic compensation system that can fit any company anywhere. Rather, you are designing a compensation system for a specific company and its specific business strategy and context. As you read FastCat's history and its plan for moving forward, be alert for the unique circumstances the company faces.

As in the real world, you will discover that your classmates may look at the same circumstances at FastCat and make different decisions. Much can be learned by explaining your decisions and understanding why your classmates made different ones.

At first you may ask, "What does my instructor want?" Many students are uneasy because the steps are not laid out in detail for each decision. This is deliberate. You are not being asked to feed back what is in the textbook. Instead, think about what you have read and the situation FastCat faces, and then apply your knowledge. As your experience and understanding increase, so will your ability to achieve the results you want with your decisions. Read the related chapters in your textbook before you begin each phase to get a better sense of how the decisions in each phase fit the overall compensation plan.

FASTCAT'S HISTORY

"The right care, at the right time and easy access to my health information." That's how one satisfied patient reacted at Memorial Clinic. She was able to make her appointment online, her medical records and description of symptoms were available on-line to her physician during her appointment, and she could see her blood test results on a protected web site later the same day. She could even graph changes in them over time.

Before giving her a new prescription, her physician was able to check online for the latest information on any interactions with drugs she was presently taking.

This patient's reactions are typical of patients whose health care providers use the medical communication software provided by FastCat. FastCat was founded in 2001 by three engineers in Minnesota who found themselves unemployed as a result of the dot com bust. All three had worked on cutting edge projects for different software companies. Pooling their experience and ideas, they identified a niche that they believed was underserved: healthcare support software for small and medium-sized medical facilities. They believed that this market was likely to be profitable relatively quickly, as the potential productivity gains for users could be substantial. Before companies like FastCat provided such software products, processes for communicating patient information among health care providers, physicians and patients were fragmented and frustrating for everyone. Health care providers were frustrated with the rising costs of tracking patient medical data and filing insurance claims. One group of doctors even tracked the reams of paper they had to read just to get background on the patients they saw during clinic hours. Patients were frustrated about seeing doctors who could only fleetingly review their medical history right before entering the examination room. Getting back test results was equally frustrating; call a week after the test, then wait for the doctor or nurse to return your call. To get a complete picture of the care a patient was receiving was time-consuming and expensive for everyone. There was also little ability to use data to make better health care decisions.

Minnesota has a long history of physician – engineering partnerships; Medtronic, St. Jude Medical, and many other medical device companies have started there. So it was not too difficult to find several medical practices that were willing to work with the engineers to develop and field test their new software. While the objective of the software sounds simple—provide the right information to the right people at the right time to ensure the right care—the software itself is not simple. Medical information is complex and varied; it includes diagnostic images and laboratory results often produced by outside facilities. Procedures and information required for billing and insurance reimbursement vary by providers and by patients. Plus, privacy must be safeguarded at every step in the process. Web sites and internal screens must be friendly to a wide variety of users. FastCat software streamlines the information flow, improves data reporting, and helps ensure accurate treatment. It helps eliminate process inefficiencies that are expensive to maintain and of no value to either the patient or the physician.

A study done at one site found that "patients are more satisfied with their care and communicate better with their doctors" when the physician uses the technology to share information with the patient. As one patient commented, "Now, the doctor is always in."

Today, FastCat, a privately held company, has grown to 200 employees with revenues of $36.5 million and net income of $8.9 million. By focusing on leveraging information technology to improve care at small and medium-sized facilities, FastCat entered markets overlooked and underserved by larger companies. Behemoths such as IBM, Oracle and SAP provide comprehensive enterprise software systems for companies in any industry, not just health care. Other companies, such as Epic Systems, McKesson, Cerner, and Siemens Healthcare, focus specifically on healthcare software systems. These companies too are much larger than FastCat, with each having more than $1 billion in annual revenues and more than 5,000 employees. Epic Systems, for example, had revenues of $1.2 billion last year, 5,225 employees, and 260 "large" customers. If we divide that $1.2 billion in revenues by 260 customers, we find that the average Epic Systems customer spends $4.6 million per year on Epic's products and services. One of the largest Epic customers is Kaiser Permanente, which has annual revenues of $44.2 billion, operates 36 hospitals and 533 medical offices and has 167,000 employees (including over 15,000 physicians). Kaiser expects to spend roughly $4 billion on Epic products/services over a 10 to 15 year period. However, such systems and such costs are way too expensive for FastCat customers and way too complex. Because it has kept its focus on the patient-physician interface in ways that improve patient care, FastCat has built a reputation for some of the best medical software available today and it has built a customer base of smaller providers not served by the very large healthcare software companies.

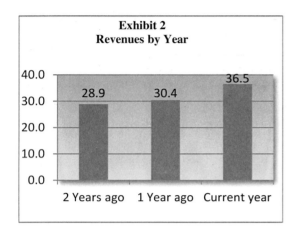

Exhibit 2
Revenues by Year

(bar chart: 2 Years ago = 28.9, 1 Year ago = 30.4, Current year = 36.5; y-axis 0.0 to 40.0)

TODAY'S NEW REALITY

"The elephants are trying to sit on us!" That is how Sonja Elian, one of the original founders and a Senior Fellow, describes the increased competition that FastCat faces today. Partially as a result of FastCat's success, the likes of IBM, Oracle and SAP are adapting their products for medium and even small medical providers. Elian believes that FastCat can win the challenge. "We are more nimble. The big guys claim they customize their software and services to meet the customers' needs, but all they do is tweak their standard packages." While FastCat is definitely smaller, it is clearly focused on providing web and mobile software and services to health providers and their patients. But those giant competitors not only offer software platforms, they also excel at offering services such as technical training for clients or even outsourcing a client's entire information technology function. "You concentrate on patient care and we will support you with our care of your information technology," they promise. And that promise has some appeal to overworked physicians and staff.

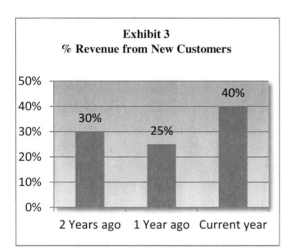

Exhibit 3
% Revenue from New Customers

(bar chart: 2 Years ago = 30%, 1 Year ago = 25%, Current year = 40%; y-axis 0% to 50%)

Ratio of Revenue to Employment Costs

FastCat had been feeling the heat. While FastCat recently expanded its head count to about 200 employees to better serve its client base and capitalize on growth in the industry, its revenue growth, while improved (see **Exhibit 2**), so far has not been as strong as hoped. Customers facing their own financial pressures are telling FastCat representatives that they need more concrete proof that the FastCat software will be a better investment than that offered by FastCat's competitors.

FastCat founders realized that they must now not only be more innovative in their approach to current customers, but must also reach out to new ones in order to boost revenue growth. **Exhibit 3** shows that most of FastCat's revenues come from existing customers. The percentage of total revenues generated by new customers has increased of late, but the question is whether it is high enough. If not, what can be done to increase it?

Very importantly, FastCat and its competitors suddenly find themselves looking at a major boom in business and revenues and even more growth may come in the near future. Why? The answer is the Health Information Technology for Economic and Clinical Health (HITECH) Act. The HITECH Act, part of the American Recovery and Reinvestment Act of 2009 (ARRA), provides the U.S. Department of Health and Human Services (HHS) with the authority to establish programs to improve health care quality, safety, and efficiency through the promotion of health information technology (HIT), including electronic health records (EHR). In fact, HITECH established an incentive program (with roughly $30 billion in funds) for health care providers to adopt, implement, upgrade or demonstrate meaningful use of certified EHR technology.[1] What's more, if they do not comply by 2015 with standards for EMR established under HITECH, they will not only miss out on the incentive payments, they will also begin to experience financial penalties via reduced Medicare reimbursement payments. So, health care providers, big and small, are moving quickly to implement (or upgrade) EHR. Even if they have an EHR is already in place, it may or may not satisfy HHS standards. So, major new spending will be required in many cases to bring current EHR systems up to standard. In summary, health care providers will receive monetary incentives, avoid eventual penalties (if they do not meet standards), and hopefully provide better health care as a result of HITECH. To do so, they will need to invest in health care technology/software.

How much growth can FastCat's industry expect? According to most projections...a lot. For example, a report by market research firm, Frost & Sullivan, finds that total market revenue for EHRs has already doubled from 2009 to 2010 alone and it projects six-fold (from $973 million to $6.5 billion) growth by 2012. At the same time, there are important notes of caution for small companies like FastCat. Larger hospitals are purchasing smaller hospitals and smaller physician practices, the kinds of customers FastCat now serves. In these cases, hospital executives may look to reduce the number of vendors they have to deal with to simplify things, to get better pricing, and to allow them to focus more on providing health care to patients. In some cases, dealing with just a single, large vendor may be seen as the solution. This trend is a major potential threat to FastCat. In addition, as one company noted in a recent annual report to investors, "Competition in the market for clinical information systems is intense, and increased government spending may entice more companies to enter the marketplace."[2] Indeed, shortly thereafter, Microsoft and General Electric announced their joint health care information technology venture, "Caradigm."

The question for FastCat is: how can it best position itself to take advantage of the tremendous growth in the industry while recognizing that its competition will be looking to do the same and that its largest competitors will be all too happy to help smaller companies like FastCat become a historical footnote? Also, FastCat must decide how much priority to give to growth as opposed to cost discipline. Growth, without keeping an eye cost control, runs the risk of FastCat's products and services becoming too expensive for its customers. Even if customers are less sensitive to costs in the next few years because of the urgency to implement/upgrade EHR software brought on by HITECH/ARRA, at some point, the tremendous industry growth will be followed by the inevitable consolidation and shake-out of companies once things return to "normal." FastCat must make sure its cost structure allows it to weather that coming storm and be a competitive company going forward from that point.

FastCat must also assess how the substantial industry growth will affect the labor market for key employee skills that FastCat needs. How much will hiring increase in the industry? If everyone increases their hiring, what kind of pressure will that put on salary and total compensation levels? Are there certain core job/skill areas that will be especially critical for FastCat? What will it take for FastCat to recruit and retain enough talented employees to take advantage of the expanding demand for EHR and related products in the industry? Will FastCat find that its better people increasingly get courted by competitors? What will FastCat be able to accomplish if gets its pay strategy right and what might happen if FastCat gets it wrong? Making "seat of the pants" or ad hoc compensation decisions is starting to look like an approach that FastCat can ill afford and which may put it at risk.

In response to this new reality in the competitive environment, the founders and several key employees formed the "New Reality" team to assess what is right at FastCat, what is wrong, and where the company needs to go in light of current conditions. The assessment covered financial conditions, customer expectations, and the quality of FastCat's engineering and marketing talent.

---

[1] ARRA 2009 specifies three main components of Meaningful Use: (1) The use of a certified EHR in a meaningful manner, such as e-prescribing. (2) The use of certified EHR technology for electronic exchange of health information to improve quality of health care. (3) The use certified EHR technology to submit clinical quality and other measures.
https://www.cms.gov/EHRIncentivePrograms/30 Meaningful Use.asp#BOOKMARK1

[2] United States Securities and Exchange Commission. Form 10-K Mediware Information Systems, inc. Filed July 9, 2011

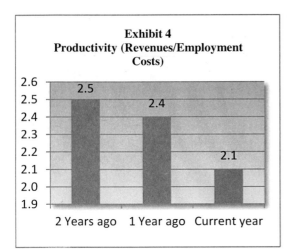

Exhibit 4
Productivity (Revenues/Employment Costs)

- 2 Years ago: 2.5
- 1 Year ago: 2.4
- Current year: 2.1

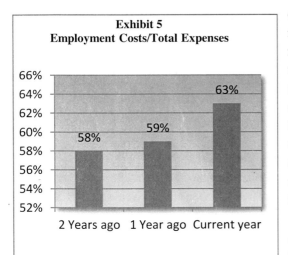

Exhibit 5
Employment Costs/Total Expenses

- 2 Years ago: 58%
- 1 Year ago: 59%
- Current year: 63%

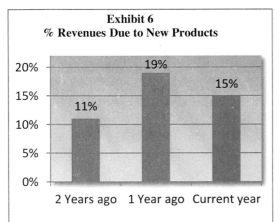

Exhibit 6
% Revenues Due to New Products

- 2 Years ago: 11%
- 1 Year ago: 19%
- Current year: 15%

TODAY'S NEW REALITY: FINANCIAL CONDITIONS

Revenue growth is a key financial metric for any company. FastCat's revenue growth and business success depend on the talents of its people. Its recent workforce growth seems to have contributed to a rebound in revenue growth. However, the recent expansion of its work force has also translated into lower productivity (revenue/employment costs, **Exhibit 4**) and into employment costs becoming a larger percentage of total expenses (**Exhibit 5**). Nevertheless, FastCat's software continues to have a reputation for outstanding quality and high reliability and FastCat wants to have enough employees in place to capitalize on growth opportunities. The founders believe "the 'Cat' is bouncing back"—it is rekindling revenue growth. Now, it needs to improve productivity, even as it recognizes that some inefficiencies are often inevitable during a period of rapid growth and hiring. To do so, FastCat must become more strategic in its approach to markets and customers. FastCat's leaders are pursuing a three-pronged strategy. One part is to drill deeper into its current client base with new products. Another is to expand the base to new categories of participants in health care. The third is to expand into new geographic markets. **Exhibit 6** shows the percentage of FastCat revenues attributed to new products. There is room for growth here. The New Reality team sees innovation as critical to sustain its advantage over competitors. FastCat hopes to deepen its client base with several new products that are just coming out, including one called "Your Doctor Makes House Calls." "House Calls" is software that automatically calls elderly/infirm patients every day and asks them a series of questions in order to assess their health. If patients do not answer, respond to questions in unusual ways, or if they request assistance, a medical staff is alerted to follow up. Doctors can sign up patients for this service, or a family member may request it.

Another new product focuses on the physician. "Facts at Your Finger Tips" is an application that permits doctors to update themselves on the very latest research related to specific conditions. It makes practicing medicine based on research evidence more feasible. It even has an expert system embedded in the software that suggests "Best Practices"—recommended treatments—based on symptoms and patient history. "Finger Tips" also offers physicians summaries of recent research related to their specialties. Finally, FastCat has developed mobile apps ("Mobile Care") that allow patients to access their health information (e.g., recent blood pressure readings, test results, appointments) and physicians on the go to access patient health records easily and quickly. Finger Tips", "House Calls", "Mobile Care" and other products under development are aimed at not only deepening the relationships with existing customers and adding to revenues, but also attracting new categories of customers, such as physicians in a solo and/or small practices. This is the "Expand Sideways" part of the FastCat strategy.

The third part of the strategy is to begin to take its products nationwide and explore its international potential. To date the majority of FastCat customers are in the Midwestern United States. Health care providers from other countries are looking at the feasibility of adapting components of FastCat's software for their unique situations. FastCat has formed a team to identify initial international sites to field test its software under local conditions. This team may also choose to consider whether certain types of work (e.g., programming) currently done by U.S. FastCat employees can be done with the same quality, but at a lower cost overseas and closer to overseas customers.

As part of these new initiatives, FastCat is also ramping up its Application Services and Management Solutions. This involves training programs for medical staff, physicians, as well as patients. On-line tutorials will allow everyone to understand what information is available to them and how to get it. Sonja Elian reports "We are taking a page from these big competitors. Applications management, training and updating are high-margin, very profitable parts of the business." FastCat is expanding its services to help insure that its software tools remain high value to customers and their patients. FastCat is beginning to write long-term contracts to provide services for users of its software applications.

TODAY'S NEW REALITY: FASTCAT EMPLOYEES

Because of the importance of its engineering and marketing talent, members of the "New Reality" team visited key individuals in this group to assure them of their continued importance at FastCat and to solicit their ideas for FastCat's future directions.

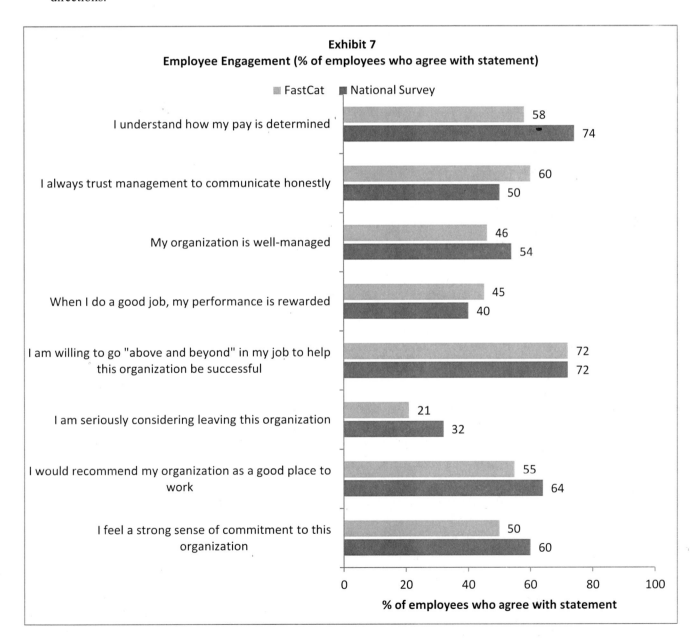

Exhibit 7
Employee Engagement (% of employees who agree with statement)

■ FastCat ■ National Survey

Statement	FastCat	National Survey
I understand how my pay is determined	58	74
I always trust management to communicate honestly	60	50
My organization is well-managed	46	54
When I do a good job, my performance is rewarded	45	40
I am willing to go "above and beyond" in my job to help this organization be successful	72	72
I am seriously considering leaving this organization	21	32
I would recommend my organization as a good place to work	55	64
I feel a strong sense of commitment to this organization	50	60

% of employees who agree with statement

All those interviewed agreed that the company's future is closely tied to the quality of its software engineering and marketing talent. FastCat believes its talent is the cream of the crop, and it wants it to stay that way. At its core, it is a technology company with a commitment to providing its customers with high-value software on time and on budget. It must maintain this reputation as it goes forward.

FastCat has always sought to hire individuals who are flexible and innovative enough to accept change. Employees possess strong problem solving skills, initiative, and ingenuity. Entry level technicians can be hired with little or no prior work experience, but they must demonstrate strong math and interpersonal skills. Engineers usually have several years of experience before FastCat hires them. Because of the specialized nature of its software, FastCat prefers to promote people from within FastCat to higher-level jobs rather than from outside, as internal candidates will already be familiar with FastCat products and its client base.

The individual interviews were followed up with company-wide surveys to measure the depth of feelings and solicit suggestions on focusing employees toward the future. Part of the survey results are shown in **Exhibit 7**. To put the responses in context, the HR manager borrowed some items from a recent Mercer survey on "employee engagement." According to a Mercer press release, "In today's demanding business environment, employers want employees who are not just satisfied, but truly engaged in their work and the success of the organization. We characterize engaged employees as those who feel a vested interest in their employers' success and who perform at levels that exceed their stated job requirements. These employees willingly contribute discretionary effort that helps to drive business performance and establish a source of competitive advantage."

FastCat employees (who call themselves 'Cats') do not seem to be as "engaged" as the owners would like. Only 50% said they felt "a strong sense of commitment to this organization," as opposed to 60% agreement in a U.S. sample. Also of concern, 21% say they are seriously considering leaving FastCat. However, that is lower than the national average of 32%. So, framed more positively, indicates that most (79%) FastCat employees are not looking to leave. (It would be relevant to know which 21% it is that is thinking of leaving.) Another positive survey result is that most (72%) of Cats agree that they are "willing to go 'above and beyond' in my job to help this organization be successful." Nevertheless, the percentage of FastCat employees who say they understand how their pay is determined, that good performance is rewarded, and that the organization is well-managed is lower than FastCat might wish.

Employee Attitudes: What Do the FastCats Think?

In the comments section of the survey, employees said they understood that changes were necessary. In fact, they welcome change and expressed strong interest in becoming involved. However, they are now uncertain about what they should be doing to help FastCat succeed. One even described FastCat as having "already lived seven of its nine lives; the most fun is already behind us." Others worry that the competition is going to "run over us." Yet employees feel very proud of how FastCat software has helped doctors care for their patients. They especially like hearing positive reactions about the software from patients and physicians. This clearly makes the FastCats "feel like we are making contributions through our work." But they are uncertain about the future. "Where are we going from here?" and "what is FastCat's plan for the near term and longer term?" In spite of some dissatisfaction in some areas, employees are proud of the reputation FastCat has for its innovative software. They believe FastCat products do help their customers provide better health care. They are enthused about the creativity of their coworkers and the company's innovative applications. However, they remain wary about its growth prospects under current economic conditions and the future directions of FastCat.

TODAY'S NEW REALITY: CUSTOMER VIEWS

The last part of the "New Reality" team's information gathering was visits and surveys to all its customers. The results, **Exhibit 8**, show the good news. FastCat customers continue to be pleased with the software as well as the FastCat representatives they have contact with. In spite of employee uncertainty over FastCat's direction, it is clear that FastCat is trying to serve its customers. Customers describe FastCat representatives as "responsive and knowledgeable" and as trustworthy. Most importantly, customers definitely feel that the FastCat software adds value. One doctor commented that he is able to see more patients and have greater confidence in his decisions when he used the software. Another doctor who piloted "Facts at your Fingertips" said that she particularly liked being able to compare her recommendations for patient treatment with what outside experts recommended. A third doctor said, "At last, it is easier and faster to get a complete look at what's going on with my patients." On the other hand, FastCat customers have questions about the cost of FastCat's products and some have concerns about the time it takes to get FastCat products up and running smoothly.

Finally, using other data, FastCat has analyzed its revenue sources. FastCat discovered that it is maintaining some customers who generate high costs relative to project revenues. For a variety of reasons (often related to the quality of their employees), these customers consistently require more resources from FastCat. The contracts that were signed may have been necessary to get these customers on board, but they are contributing little or nothing to FastCat's profits. They must be restructured to make them worth the resources FastCat is devoting to them, or they must be "fired." A new approach to service contracting may solve this issue.

FASTCAT BUSINESS STRATEGY: THE CAT COMES BACK

Concepts such as the Balanced Scorecard highlight the importance of employee and customer attitudes as important leading indicators and drivers of future financial performance. FastCat too sees its relationships with customers and employees as keys to its future success. The "New Reality" team's recommendations to "Drill Deeper" into its existing customer base with new offerings

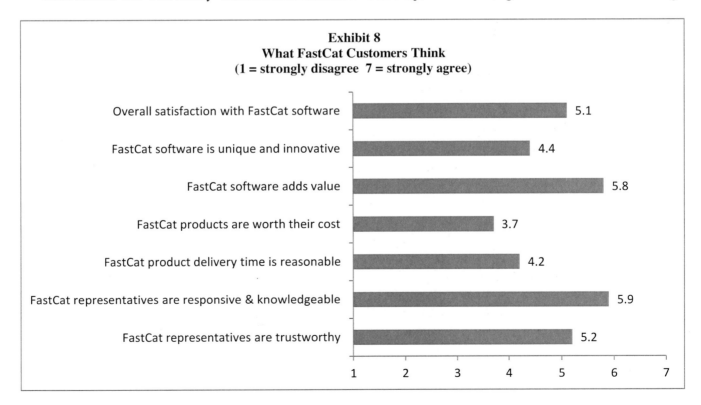

Exhibit 8
What FastCat Customers Think
(1 = strongly disagree 7 = strongly agree)

Overall satisfaction with FastCat software	5.1
FastCat software is unique and innovative	4.4
FastCat software adds value	5.8
FastCat products are worth their cost	3.7
FastCat product delivery time is reasonable	4.2
FastCat representatives are responsive & knowledgeable	5.9
FastCat representatives are trustworthy	5.2

and service contracts, "Expand Sideways" with new customers, and "Expand Territory" nationwide, even globally, are exciting and challenging. Today's healthcare practices demand greater efficiency, increased productivity, stricter accountability, tighter security and more rigorous cost containment. FastCat has software that it feels meets these demands. The major new incentives put in place by the HITECH/ARRA legislation to spur EHR meaningful use provide a tremendous opportunity for FastCat to move to a new level in its industry.

All parts of the FastCat strategy require a great deal of creativity from the engineering and marketing staff. They also require close collaboration between marketing and engineering so that engineers are not producing products that do not have a ready market. Marketing people must better understand how to broaden applications and services within current customers. They must also begin to sell the software in new territories. They must figure out ways to help FastCat customers operate more efficiently so that FastCat makes more money. Right now, engineers still develop products for each customer pretty much in isolation, with only limited discussions with either marketing people or directly with customers. The technicians test the systems and focus on quality assurance. Finance, marketing and sales are involved later in the process. The New Reality team believes that interaction with current and potential clients will help the engineering staff better understand and be responsive to the market. So the relationship and work flow between marketing, engineering, and technical employees need attention.

FastCat leaders know that even though current and potential customers will be increasing their spending on EHR/meaningful use compliant software, the competition will continue to be fierce. The marketing message is, "We deliver cost-effective solutions to make medical care providers more productive at every step of the way." The message to employees is, "every single one of us must be vigilant in both driving revenue and managing costs. We must be sure our cash reserves are directed to our business objectives. We remain committed to creating value for our customers."

Employees must be re-energized and refocused on the new strategic directions. According to the New Reality team report, "Too many people are looking in the rear-view mirror." "People continue to look back at the high-flying early years instead of looking ahead to FastCat's future." FastCat needs highly committed employees who work together to support improved health care for its customers' patients. To do that, all employees must share the vision of where the company intends to go. A new mission statement, shown in **Exhibit 9**, has been sent to all employees. It is called the "Partnership for Success." FastCat believes its emphasis on teamwork and innovation will put its three-prong strategy into practice.

YOUR FIRST PROJECT AT FASTCAT: RECOMMEND OBJECTIVES

Congratulations! FastCat was extremely impressed by your employment interview, and wants you to start today as their first compensation specialist. Chapters 1 and 2 of the *Compensation* textbook, this casebook, classroom discussion, and your instructor will be your sources of information to complete this project. FastCat knows it needs a compensation system that will reflect its changing strategic direction and vision and help the company succeed.

COMPENSATION AT FASTCAT

Think about FastCat's present and future. What factors in its business environment (Competitive pressure? Regulatory pressure?—See HITECH/ARRA and EHR/meaningful use. Labor market pressure? Changing customer needs? Others?) are impinging on FastCat today? What factors are likely to become more important (or less important) in the future? How should FastCat respond? What is FastCat's business strategy? How does FastCat plan to compete? Information on these first two issues is found in FastCat history. The New Reality team has identified a number of pressures and laid out a business strategy, in light of those pressures. What is FastCat's HR philosophy? What are the company's values? How must the compensation system be consistent with these values? How can it communicate and reinforce these values? Be sure you consider what the Reality team says in its message to employees about the Partnership for Success.

Exhibit 9
FastCat's Mission Statement

FASTCAT'S MISSION:
A PARTNERSHIP FOR SUCCESS

To exceed our customer's expectations of value, dependability and reliability by focusing on innovation and teamwork; to help our customers succeed; to support and share with our employees; and to respect and recognize individuals and their performance contributions.

The key to our success is our Partnership among customers and all FastCat employees. Together, we can maintain the innovation and enthusiasm that have served FastCat so well.

We measure our success by our customers' success.

We must produce innovative, high-quality solutions and unsurpassed service to our customers that our competitors will find impossible to match. These solutions will be designed in collaboration with our customers.

Individual employees remain the heart of FastCat. Each one of us makes a difference.

Together, we work as a team.

Our customers are part of this team to deliver cutting-edge solutions.

Innovative solutions depend on each of us, the FastCat cadre.

It is too soon to propose specific compensation practices. However, what is necessary at this point is to **recommend a set of objectives** that supports FastCat business strategy and that you think FastCat should be able to achieve with the compensation system you are about to design.

OBJECTIVES FOR FASTCAT'S COMPENSATION SYSTEM

Combine what you know about FastCat's business strategy and your analysis to recommend compensation objectives for FastCat. You should consider:

- **FastCat's Performance**. Profits, revenue growth, customer satisfaction—should they be in your objectives?

- **FastCat's Employment Costs**. Do the trends in the cost ratios in Exhibits 4 and 5 raise any concerns?

- **FastCat Employee Attitudes and Behaviors**. Turn back to the customer and employee survey information in Exhibits 7 and 8. Should FastCat use pay to influence employee behaviors? What behaviors are vital to FastCat's business strategy? Where do people's decision to join, stay, and work smarter (attract, retain, motivate) fit?

- **Legal Compliance**. How should FastCat manage pay in light of laws and regulations? (At this stage, we have not said much about legal issues. However, it is important to keep this consideration in mind.)

- **Role of Compensation**. Should FastCat's compensation system be a source of sustainable competitive advantage? Or should it only support other strategic initiatives? If it is to be a source of competitive advantage, it must go beyond aligning with FastCat's business. It must **differentiate** FastCat from its competitors and **be difficult for competitors to copy**. (Of course, differentiation must create value and truly support the strategy. Just being different alone is not the path to competitive advantage or even competitive parity.)

The objectives you propose will guide you as you design FastCat's pay system. A generic set of objectives not tailored to FastCat might be "to cost effectively attract, retain, and motivate a competent workforce and comply with regulations." But do not just copy these objectives for FastCat. Instead, specify objectives that reflect FastCat's situation.

Keep in mind that:

*The compensation **objectives** specify WHAT you wish to achieve with your pay system.*

*The compensation **strategy** specifies HOW FastCat will achieve these objectives.*

The pay system translates the strategy into practice.

***Objectives become the standards** you can use to judge the success of the pay system that you recommended.*

Ask Your Instructor

Some instructors ask students for written reports on their compensation objectives for FastCat. Others ask students to include them in their Phase I report. Some instructors also discuss them in class. At the minimum, be sure to include them and your explanation of why you are recommending them as part of your first assignment. You will be building on them as the term progresses. Be sure that you are able to specify how the objectives you propose:

(1) address the compensation implications of FastCat's environment;

(2) support FastCat's business strategy; and

(3) reflect FastCat's values.

PHASE I

INTERNAL

ALIGNMENT:

Determining the Structure

In Phase I you will look at the descriptions of a sample of jobs at FastCat and decide how to arrange them into a structure. Make these decisions based on what you know about Fast-Cat's work flows, its business strategy, and its values. The structure you recommend and the plan to create it should help FastCat achieve the objectives you recommended earlier.

As you work on Phase I, continually ask the questions, "How will my decision help FastCat compete? How will it affect FastCat employees and customers?" The point is to not only understand "how" to design a pay plan but more importantly "why" your recommendation makes sense.

A road map for your work in Phase I is on the next page. Refer to it as you work through the assignment.

PHASE I (Internal Structure) STEPS:

Step 1: Recommend Strategy and Objectives

A. How will your internal structure strategy support objectives?
B. How detailed/tailored versus flexible is your recommended structure?
C. How hierarchical versus flat is your recommended structure?

Step 2: Recommend an Internal Structure

If You Recommended a <u>Job</u>-Based Internal Structure:

A. Describe the process used to design the plan.
B. Specify whether you recommend a single versus multiple structures.
C. Describe your plan. What compensable factors & weights are used and how do these relate to business strategy, work, and values?
D. Apply your plan to the jobs and describe your resulting structure. Use a "picture" (i.e., an exhibit) to show your structure. If you used point-based job evaluation, show the hierarchy of jobs based on their job evaluation points (total and for each compensable factor).
E. Evaluate your job-based structure and evaluate whether it will be successful in executing your recommended strategy and achieving your recommended objectives.

If You Recommend a <u>Person</u>-based Internal Structure:

A. Describe the process used to design the plan.
B. Specify whether you recommend a single versus multiple structures.
C. Describe your plan.
D. Apply your plan to the jobs and describe your resulting structure. Use a "picture" (i.e., an exhibit) to show your structure. The picture of your recommended structure should show skill blocks or competencies, their levels, and how they are weighted.
E. Evaluate your person-based structure and evaluate whether it will be successful in executing your recommended strategy and achieving your recommended objectives.

Step 3: Recommend an Implementation Plan

A. Include a manual with enough information to apply the plan.
B. How will the structure be maintained over time? Is there flexibility to change?
C. How will the process and communication issues be managed?

BACKGROUND

Chapters 3 through 6 of the *Compensation* textbook discuss the need for internal alignment in a pay system. ***Internal alignment means that FastCat work forms a structure based on factor(s) that are important for FastCat's success.*** The structure that results from this alignment will serve as one basis for pay decisions in Phase II.

The ***number of levels*** and the ***criteria*** used to determine the levels help form the internal structure. Because internal structures are meant to reflect the organization design and the flow of work, some are more hierarchical with multiple levels compared to others which are flatter with fewer levels. Structures typically pay more for work that requires greater knowledge to perform, generates results that are more valued, and is performed under less desirable working conditions. The criteria used to determine the number of levels can be either job-based (job evaluation) or person-based (skill/competency). Keep in mind that you will be determining the pay rates for the structure in Phase II.

Exhibit 10 shows an organization that uses four different structures. Each is created using separate criteria in separate plans. A job evaluation plan was used for the administrative work. A different job evaluation plan, using different compensable factors, was used for the manufacturing group. Person-based plans were used for the technical group (skill-based) and managerial employees (competencies). The result of these four plans is the internal structure shown in **Exhibit 10**. Another compensation manager might have used fewer plans to simplify the bureaucracy and as shown in **Exhibit 10**, created a flatter structure with fewer levels.

How Will I Know Internal Alignment When I See It?

According to Chapter 3 of the *Compensation* textbook, a well-aligned structure supports the work flow, is fair to employees, and directs their behaviors toward organization objectives. "Fair to employees" implies equal pay for equal or similar work and acceptable differentials for dissimilar work. A well-aligned structure is also easier to explain to employees, more efficient to administer, and more cost-effective. Keep these requirements in mind as you make your decisions in Phase I; use them again to judge both your *results* (the internal structure you recommend for FastCat) and your *plans* (i.e. job and or person based) in your report.

Exhibit 10 Four Structures within an Organization

MANAGERIAL Competency-based	TECHNICAL Skill-based	MANUFACT-URING Job Evaluation	SUPPORT Job Evaluation
Vice Presidents	Head/Chief Engineer	Assembler I Inspector I	Office Manager
Division General Managers	Senior Engineers	Packer	Admin Assistant
Managers	Engineers	Materials Handler Inspector II	Principal Secretary
Project Leaders	Senior Technicians	Assembler II	Word Processor II
Supervisors	Technicians	Drill Press Operator	Clerk
		Machinist I	Messenger

STEP 1: RECOMMEND STRATEGY AND OBJECTIVES

Before you began Phase I, you considered the compensation implications of FastCat's business environment and linked that environment with FastCat's business strategy and values. You took the first step to develop FastCat's compensation strategy by specifying the objectives for the compensation system.   Now, recommend a strategy on internal alignment for FastCat and explain…

A. How Will Your Recommended Structure Support the Strategy and Objectives?

You know from Chapter 2 in the *Compensation* textbook that companies may propose similar objectives but have different strategies to achieve them. So even if all your colleagues in your class recommend the same compensation objectives for FastCat, you will likely decide on different strategies and different plans (e.g. job evaluation plans with different factors) to achieve them.

Chapter 3 calls out two strategic choices: (1) how "tailored" to organization design and workflow to make the structure, and (2) how hierarchical versus flat it should be.

B. *How Tight to Tailor (How Many Structures)?*

Should detailed descriptions of the work be used to create multiple (e.g., four as in **Exhibit 10**) distinct structures with five levels? Or should work expectations be kept more fluid, with work defined as broader roles, as in **Exhibit 11** which uses three levels in (fewer) two structures? **Jump ahead to take a peek at Step 4 in Phase II. There you will find survey data showing how organizations typically use and design pay grades. Use this information to begin thinking about the number and size of grades you will recommend.**

Exhibit 11 Two Structures in the Same Organization with the Same Work

PROFESSIONAL Person-based	SUPPORT Job Evaluation
Level 3	Band 3
Level 2	Band 2
Level 1	Band 1

Which approach will help FastCat achieve its compensation objectives? What will best support its business strategy? Which approach will support employee movement and career paths within FastCat? Which approach will convince FastCat employees that they are being treated equitably?

The advantage of a tightly tailored structure based on detailed descriptions is that it can help reduce uncertainty about what is expected of employees. (Plus, it provides work for job analysts.) Is this what FastCat needs? A more loosely tailored structure allows more fluidity in work assignments but risks separating what employees are actually doing from the description of work. Will a tightly (or loosely) tailored structure help FastCat satisfy its customers and generate revenues?

C. *Hierarchical versus Flat?*

Your answers to these questions will be a matter of degree. It is not either/or. Thinking about these questions may help you place your Phase I decisions within the broader perspective of the entire human resource management system. Keep focused on how to support FastCat's strategic goals—how to help FastCat win.

Describe how your internal alignment strategy will help FastCat meet the compensation objectives you already called out. Use the examples in the *Compensation* textbook as guides. Be sure to include a statement of your Internal Alignment Strategy and your rationale for recommending it.

STEP 2: RECOMMEND AN INTERNAL STRUCTURE

…What you discuss here depends on whether you are recommending a job-based versus a person-based structure….

FOR JOB-BASED STRUCTURES:

In practice, the process of creating an internal structure starts with job analysis that describes the similarities and differences in work within the organization. That step has already been done. The results are the *FastCat job descriptions that begin at this end of this chapter*. Although there are more than these jobs at FastCat, these are the only ones to use in your analysis. However, keep in mind that this is *not a representative sample.* That is, you cannot draw conclusions about the number of engineering jobs versus the number of marketing jobs at FastCat based on their proportions in the sample.

A. Process Used to Design the Job-Based Plan

If you involve other groups of FastCat employees or managers in designing your plan, tell the nature of that involvement, and what purpose it will serve. The *Compensation* textbook discusses who might be involved in the process.

B. Single versus Multiple Plans

The sample of FastCat jobs covers at least four job families: engineering, marketing, technical and administrative work. You have three different options for building an internal structure at FastCat. One is a single structure that includes all job families and uses the same plan to evaluate all jobs. Or, you could create two structures. One structure might include engineers and technicians and another one marketing and administration. You could even use four structures with a different plan for each job family. The organization in **Exhibit 10** uses four structures, **Exhibit 11** shows two structures.

A single plan may seem the least bureaucratic and communicate a common value system. But a single plan may not adequately evaluate all positions. You may also find in Phase II that it makes it harder to compare pay rates in the market. Four structures may seem the best way to be sure all jobs are accurately described on factors that are important and specific to the work. But ***structures create boundaries.*** Each structure creates another boundary within FastCat. So each boundary you create should add value to FastCat. FastCat faces different external market conditions for engineers. Plus, they are vital to the company's strategy. So it may make sense to propose a separate structure for engineers. Do any other job families require separate structures? Keep in mind that the enhanced ability to attract and retain key talent (engineers, marketers) must be enough to offset the increased bureaucracy created by the additional boundaries.

If you decide that more than one plan makes sense, you may wish to use a person-based structure (based on competencies and/or skills) for part of the work at FastCat. That option is discussed below. If time permits, this project offers a low-risk opportunity to gain some experience with person-based structures. However, many teams will not have time to do this. Be sure to check with your instructor before you recommend such structures.

How to Decide What Makes Sense for FastCat?

The following questions will help you decide whether to use a single or multiple plans. *(You do NOT need to answer all these questions in your written report. They are included to help guide your thinking in making your recommendations.)*

What strategy did you recommend for internal alignment? Did you recommend "tight" tailoring, or a more fluid approach? How does the number of plans relate to hierarchy? Think through the implications of your alignment strategy on the number of plans to use.

Think about FastCat's business strategy. It depends heavily on engineering and marketing. Will putting engineering in the same plan with administrative jobs make it easier or harder for FastCat to keep its focus on engineering?

Think about the compensation objectives you specified. Do they lead to any conclusions about the number of plans to use?

C. Describe your Job-Based Plan

Job-based plans vary in their complexity and in what factors in the job are to be used as a basis of evaluation. The *Compensation* textbook lists the advantages and disadvantages of various approaches to creating a job-based plan. Remember that the point of your plan is to identify similarities and differences in the content of the work. Are these differences that FastCat should pay for? Be sure that the differences and similarities your plan identifies are the right ones for FastCat.

Exhibit 12 Defining and Scaling a Compensable Factor

Factor: Mental Demands
Definition: *The mental capacity to perform the given job, expressed in resourcefulness in dealing with unfamiliar problems, interpretation of data*

DEGREE	POINT VALUE	DESCRIPTION OF CHARACTERISTICS
1	25	Seldom confronts problems not covered by job routine or organization policy; analysis of data is negligible.
2	50	Follows clearly prescribed standard practices and involves straightforward application of readily understood rules and procedures. Analyzes non-complicated data by established routine.
3	75	Frequently confronts problems not covered by job routine. Independent judgment exercised in making minor decisions where alternatives are limited and standard policies are established. Analysis of standardized data for information of or use by others.
4	100	Exercises independent judgment in making decisions involving non-routine problems with general guidance only from higher supervision. Analyzes and evaluates data pertaining to non-routine problems for solution in conjunction with others.
5	125	Uses independent judgment in making decisions that are subject to review in the final stages only. Analyzes and solves non-routine problems involving evaluation of a wide variety of data as a regular part of job duties. Makes decisions involving procedures.
6	150	Uses independent judgment in making decisions that are not subject to review. Regularly exercises developmental or creative ability in policy development.

Describe your plan(s) in detail. If you use compensable factors, define them; tell how you chose them, how you scaled them, and how you weighted them. **Exhibit 12** defines and scales the compensable factor Mental Demands.

The following section provides some additional help in developing compensable factors. But be sure to check Chapter 5 in the *Compensation* textbook for more detail on designing a job evaluation plan.

1. Choose Compensable Factors

Compensable factors reflect how work adds value to the organization. They flow from the work itself (*see the job descriptions at the end of this phase*) and the strategic direction of the business (*see the earlier introductory material about FastCat*).

a. Consider FastCat's Business Strategy and Values

FastCat's executives are the best source of information on the company's business strategy, values, etc. Re-read those sections of the casebook to glean possible compensable factors. What does FastCat value? For example, does FastCat achieve competitive advantage through product innovation? If so, then the degree of innovation required to perform each job may be a compensable factor. After all, a good way to reinforce innovation is to signal its importance by including it in the pay system.

Look over FastCat's mission statement. What compensable factors are included in the statement? For example, FastCat's "Partnership for Success" says:

We must produce innovative, high-quality solutions....designed in collaboration with our customers.

Should compensable factors reinforce collaboration? If yes, then FastCat may want to give greater value to jobs that require greater collaboration. You may want to create a list of possible compensable factors and their sources (e.g., mission statement, business strategy, job descriptions).

b. Consider the Work Itself

What do the job descriptions stress? If the majority of them stress the importance of product quality, then responsibility for quality may be a compensable factor. If they emphasize superior job knowledge, then perhaps breadth and depth of job knowledge should be a compensable factor. Employees also provide an invaluable perspective on what they think the company values (or should value) in their jobs. Most companies have a process for employee participation.

c. Narrow your List

By now you have probably got a lengthy list of possible factors. The text discusses practical issues such as how many factors to use, how to increase acceptability, and avoiding overlap. For example, are "creativity required" and "innovation" both getting at the same thing? If they are, then using both factors will doubly reward jobs in which the factor is important.

d. Refine your Definition

Defining a compensable factor requires that you visualize the responsibilities of jobs that vary widely on the factor being considered. For example, suppose that FastCat decides that client interaction is central to its business. How does client interaction vary? To answer the question, think of three jobs that represent different points on a client interaction continuum,

e.g. administrative assistant II   project support assistant   client account leader

Now ask the question, "How does client interaction differ among these jobs? One obvious way is the *frequency* of contacts. Tracking expenses requires little client interaction. Scheduling meetings requires quite a bit.

But is frequency the only way interaction differs? For example, the project support assistant may have more contact with clients than the client account leader during the course of a single day. Would you rate the project support assistant job as high as the client account leader on client interaction? Why or why not?

Clearly, the *nature* of client interaction may make a difference. A project support assistant gives and answers simple factual questions. A client account leader must ask questions to identify client needs, persuade, negotiate, process, and resolve differences. So the type of interaction is important, too.

Exhibit 13 Sample Job Evaluation Form

Compensable Factor	Degree x Weight = Total (1 thru 5)
Working Conditions Environment Hazards	(1 2 3 4 5) x __ = __
Skill Education Experience Mental Manual/Specific	(1 2 3 4 5) x __ = __
Effort Physical Mental	(1 2 3 4 5) x __ = __
Responsibility Effort of Error Inventiveness/Innovation	(1 2 3 4 5) x __ = __

Are frequency and type of client information sufficient for your definition? The answer depends on your company. Many companies have broadened the definition of clients to include other employees within the company. For example, what is the frequency and type of interaction involving the engineering, IT, and marketing jobs? Is this interaction important to FastCat?

2. Scale the Compensable Factor

Once a factor is defined, you need to scale it. Part of this job is already done. In our example for the factor "client interaction," we have already identified as subfactors frequency and nature of contacts and whether they are internal or external. To scale factors, think of the specific jobs and how they differ on each of the subfactors. Set up a continuum on these subfactors and attach factor degrees to points on the continuum.

3. Weight the Factors Based on Their Importance

Once degrees have been chosen, defined, and scaled, factors can be weighted based on the importance of each factor. For example, each degree of client interaction may be worth two points, or 20 points, or 40 points. Chapter 5 in the *Compensation* textbook should help you with scaling and weighting factors. A sample job evaluation form is shown in **Exhibit 13**. The left column includes four compensable factors with subfactors. The column on the right allows room to circle the degree of each factor a job might contain and multiply that degree by the factor weight to arrive at the JE points for the factor. The sum for all factors gives the JE points for the job.

D. Apply your Plan to FastCat Jobs and Describe the Results   *apply w/in comp. w/in survey*

Be sure to secure approval by FastCat's top management for your proposed factors and degrees. You will increase your chances of obtaining this approval if you can clearly demonstrate how your factors are related to FastCat's business strategy.

Once you have designed your plan, apply it to the FastCat jobs in this manual. Include a <u>picture</u> (i.e., a chart) showing your resulting structure. If you used a point-based job evaluation system, your picture/chart should show all FastCat jobs, their total job evaluation points, and their job evaluation points on each compensable factor.

As you analyze the job descriptions and apply your plan, you may discover jobs that have similar content and differ by only a small number of points. These are good candidates for combining into a single job. What are the advantages to FastCat of combining jobs? What are the disadvantages? If you do combine jobs, show which ones.

E. Evaluate Your Job-Based Structure

Evaluate your structure to be sure it is consistent with FastCat's business strategy, values and compensation objectives. Is work more central to FastCat's strategic mission ranked higher? Are employee career paths clearly supported by your structure, e.g., will moving from one job to a higher one in the structure give the employee increased responsibility? What message does your structure send to employees regarding promotions, continuous learning, and flexibility?

FOR PERSON-BASED STRUCTURES:

<table>
<tr><td>

Ask Your Instructor

</td><td>

<u>*Before you begin, check with your instructor*</u> *to determine if this step is required, optional, or omitted. Not all classes will have time to design a person-based plan. If your instructor decides to omit this option, then (1) be sure all 24 jobs are included in your structure, and (2) skip to STEP THREE: IMPLEMENTING THE PLAN.*

</td></tr>
</table>

A. Process

Begin as when you developed compensable factors for your job-based structure by examining the job descriptions. Just what do you hope to accomplish with a person-based plan? Will it fit well with their business strategy? How will you gain the acceptance of people who will be paid by the plan? How will you ensure that your plan adequately captures the segment of work at FastCat that you are focusing on?

B. Single versus Multiple Plan(s)

You might recommend a skill-based approach for the technical work. Or you may wish to design a competency plan for marketing and engineering. What are the implications of such a recommendation?

C. Describe your Plan

Just as you defined and scaled compensable factors based on what you know about FastCat's values, define various levels of skill blocks or competencies. Tell how they relate to each other and to FastCat values.

1. Develop Skill Blocks or Competencies

Exhibits in the *Compensation* textbook show the links between skill categories, skill blocks, and skills, and between core competency, competency sets, and competency indicators. All of them should be derived from the organization's values, business strategy, and work.

a. Consider FastCat's business strategy and values

As with compensable factors, FastCat's mission statement is the starting place for defining core competencies. The mission statement may also help you decide whether any person-based system will help FastCat get where it says it wants to go.

b. Consider the work itself

Think about the flow of work. What skills are involved to do the work, and how do these skills build? For example, Fast-Cat engineers and technicians must prepare error-free software. So, one skill might be the ability to detect errors. How about correcting them? How about writing original code? In what programming language? Does FastCat value elegant programming, or does it emphasize getting product out the door? Does it matter?

After you have considered all the skills that are required to develop and create software, as reflected in the job descriptions, then group the skills into blocks.

As you read the job descriptions, think about the picture of FastCat that they paint. Are the job descriptions consistent with what the founders say they expect from FastCat employees? Are elements missing? For example, would a person applying for an engineering job understand the emphasis that FastCat places on teamwork and the expectations about Fast-Cat teams? There may be competencies that management says are important that are not reflected in the job descriptions. If you think so, you can recommend that the descriptions be revised. (*You are NOT expected to actually make those revisions as part of this assignment.*) However, be sure that you can link your selection of a core competence or a skill category to FastCat's business strategy and values.

c. Narrow your list

Check your list for overlap and duplication. At the same time, be sure that all major aspects of work are covered, including company-wide skills or competencies such as leadership or communication, as well as technical competencies. Keep in mind that employees focus on the behaviors for which they are paid.

d. Refine your Definition

Core competencies and skill categories should be defined so that observable behaviors can be identified that indicate the level of competency or skill. Even though competency advocates point out that the behavior reflects "underlying personal characteristics," it is the competency indicators that are used to evaluate what people are doing and build a structure. For example, the underlying personal characteristic you may be seeking is someone with a highly developed sense of ethics. But you need to translate that into observable indicators, e.g., "checks to see that terms and conditions of sales contracts are met by FastCat." "Represents FastCat software accurately." "Consults with engineering to better understand product capabilities." "Seeks opportunities for software innovation that will increase success for both FastCat and its customers." Skills are usually easier to specify as concrete behaviors. However, it is equally important for competencies to be anchored in observable behaviors.

2. Scale or Weight your Skills/Competencies

Skill-based plans are usually applied to jobs where there is a narrower range for variance, e.g., you can either identify and correct a sufficiently high percentage of software-coding errors, or you cannot. While there are differences in how efficiently the program works or the elegance of the coding, such differences may not be relevant in a skill-based plan. You will need to decide. Are degrees appropriate?

In order to apply competencies across a range of jobs, you will need to come up with behavioral indicators that will allow others to judge the degree of a competency a person possesses. **Exhibit 14** shows one student's definition and behavioral indicators for a "team orientation" competency. Notice how they clearly tie it to their compensation objectives and Fast-Cat's business strategy.

3. Develop Certification Methods

In addition to developing and defining skill blocks or core competencies, you need some way to certify that employees possess and/or are applying the skills or competencies. So be sure to design a certification procedure. Look at the exhibits in Chapter 6 of the *Compensation* textbook to see how others have presented a person-based system.

Exhibit 14 Defining a Competency

Core Competency: Team orientation

Definition: Promotes co-operation and achieves working results, which take account of the interests of all parties concerned

- Guarantees that the members of the team contribute to the result of the work and discussions

- Ensures equal treatment of team members

- Expresses recognition for contributions by team members

- Recognizes and promotes solutions that are useful to all those involved

- Promotes and finds compromises if those involved are of a different opinion

- Provides comprehensive and prompt information

- Supports team decisions even if against own opinions

D. Apply the Plan

Apply your plan to the jobs and describe your resulting structure. Use a "picture" (i.e., an exhibit) to show your structure. The picture of your recommended structure should show skill blocks or competencies, their levels, and how they are weighted.

E. Evaluate Your Results

Address the same issues you did for your job evaluation plan. How is your person-based plan consistent with FastCat's strategy, values, and business conditions? How will it help FastCat employees and customers? Check to see how employees will move through your structure. Are employee career paths clearly supported? What message does your plan send to employees regarding promotions, continuous learning, and flexibility? What are the disadvantages of person-based pay systems, and how will you minimize them?

STEP 3: IMPLEMENTING THE PLAN

Combine your job-based and (if your instructor directed you to develop it) your person-based plans and assess the entire structure for FastCat one more time. Go back to your original objectives for the compensation system. Ask yourself, *How* are your decisions consistent with those objectives? *How* will your decisions help FastCat generate solutions for its customers? *How* will they help the company compete? *How* do they signal the company's values?

Develop recommendations for how the plan is to be administered and maintained over time. Is the system flexible enough to handle new jobs or competencies as they are created? How will you gain understanding, acceptance and use of your plan? Why should managers bother with your recommendations?

Such issues as participation in the process, communication of the results, appeals procedures, overall ease of administration, reliability and validity, costs, and legal compliance are all covered in Chapter Six of the *Compensation* textbook. Address those issues you judge to be important. When you are satisfied with your work, write your report.

P. 194-200

YOUR REPORT

Executive Summary

Recommend Strategy and Objectives

Recommend Internal Structure (include a "picture")

Recommend Implementation Plan

Summary and Rationale

---

1. Executive Summary

Begin your report with an executive summary. Executive summaries capture your key recommendations and provide an overview of your report. See the example in **Exhibit 15**. You probably will write this section of your report last, after you have finalized all your recommendations. However, put this section up front in your report, right after the Table of Contents. ***Remember, an Executive Summary is NOT a Table of Contents!*** This Executive Summary need not be long – half a page will do – but it is important. It provides your "boss" a concise statement of your major recommendations.

Exhibit 15 Sample Executive Summary

> *We recommend a flexible internal structure that will help us achieve our objectives. To do this, we propose three job families: marketing, technical, and administrative/support. We propose a job-based plan for administrative/support, a competency-based plan for marketing, and a skill-based plan for technical rolls.*

2. Recommend Strategy and Objectives (Step 1 from above)

See Step 1 above. Explain how your recommended strategy will help achieve the objectives. How tightly tailored will the structure be? To what extent will it be hierarchical or flat?

3. Recommend Internal Structure. Include a picture. (Step 2 from above)

See Step 2 above. *Be sure to include an exhibit that shows your internal structure.*

1. If you used a point job evaluation plan, include the points for every factor for every job and the total points for each job. Have clear definitions of all your factors. → on excel

2. If you used a skill-based plan, include any values assigned to each skill block and level of knowledge and how the blocks are related to the work described in the job descriptions. Include the process you will use to certify that employees possess the skills.

3. If you used a competency-based plan, include your competency definitions and levels and how they relate to the job descriptions. Include your certification process.

Be very specific about how many structures you are recommending and where each FastCat job description fits in your structure. Charts and illustrations are essential.

All 25 jobs should be on 1 or 2 sheets

All of the FastCat job descriptions included in this section *must* be integrated into this structure. You may recommend reorganizing or combining some jobs. If you do, be sure to account for the original job descriptions in your exhibit. If you proposed doing away with some of the job descriptions, be sure to include a conversion chart to describe the level of skill or competence in each of the FastCat jobs. Keep track of original FastCat job titles, even if you re-title/combine/eliminate some of them, for your work in Phases II and III.

Evaluate the decisions that underlie your resulting structure:

- Are they consistent with FastCat's business strategy, compensation objectives, and your internal alignment strategy?

- Do they create a structure that supports work flow, is fair to employees, and directs employee behavior toward FastCat objectives? Include the rationale for your recommendations – how they relate to compensation objectives, and possible risks they create for FastCat.

4. Recommend Implementation Plan (Step 3 from above)

See Step 3 above. Develop recommendations for how your internal structure plan is to be administered and maintained over time. What evidence do you have regarding the reliability and validity of your plan? What are the costs? How flexible is the plan to handle new jobs and or skills/competencies? Who will participate in the process? How will the plan be communicated? How will you ensure that line managers make decisions consistent with the plan? What about appeals procedures and legal compliance?

A. Manual

Create a manual so that others can use your system. A manual permits someone other than you to understand and apply your plan and explain it to employees. With job evaluation, include details such as factors, factor definitions, weights, classification descriptions, and/or points if they are elements of your plan. If you designed a person-based plan, too, include those definitions, degrees, weights, and rationale in the same manual.

If you use any forms to assist in applying your methods, include a copy in the manual.

The exhibits and the appendixes in the textbook will provide some guidance in organizing and communicating your information. But use these exhibits for inspiration only. Build your own exhibits to reflect your own plan.

5. Summary and Rationale (This is Essential!)

Include your rationale for your recommendations. The rationale tells FastCat's top leadership (your classmates and instructor) how each recommendation will help FastCat meet its compensation objectives. This step is crucial if you want to succeed as a manager of compensation. Executives (and professors!) want to know that your recommendations are logical and clearly related to corporate objectives.

ORAL PRESENTATION

Your instructor may ask you to give an oral report to FastCat's top leadership (your classmates) on the day your assignment is due. Oral presentations serve two purposes. First, they allow comparisons of recommendations among classmates. It is always useful to see what others, given the same set of information, recommend. Second, the experience in summarizing, presenting, and evaluating proposals will help you in your post-college career. Making a presentation in the classroom is a low-risk way to gain valuable experience.

If you are asked to give an oral presentation, be sure to cover your key recommendations, along with the rationale for each.

LIST OF ALL JOBS IN FASTCAT SAMPLE

Administrative Aide

Administrative Assistant II

Administrative Leader

Client Account Leader

Clinical Liaison

Graphics Designer

Implementation Consultant

Marketing Svcs. Representative

Marketing Support

Programmer Analyst

Project Leader

Project Support Assistant

Quality Assurance Analyst

Quality Assurance Analyst A

Senior Fellow

Senior Quality Assurance Technician

Software Engineer

Software Solutions Consultant

Software User Interface Architect

Technician

Training Assistant

Travel Coordinator

User Interface Designer

Visionary Champion

FastCat Job Descriptions

ADMINISTRATIVE AIDE

Responsibilities
Prepare PowerPoint presentations at direction of other support or engineering personnel;
Enter and/or update data into FastCat databases, including but not limited to employee data such as change of address, phone number, department, location, leave of absence
Process direct deposit payroll forms
Provide word processing, faxing, copying, filing and other clerical support duties
Coordinate repair and maintenance of fax, copier, printer and other office equipment
Procure office supplies in a timely and cost-effective manner
Keep supervisor informed of changes in assignments
Other duties as assigned

Requirements
High school diploma or equivalent
Familiar with Microsoft Office application

Competencies
Work to high degree of accuracy
Willing to ask questions of others to clarify understanding of assignment
Able to communicate effectively, both written and orally
Willingness to take personal initiative in soliciting work assignments
Willing to contribute as active member of office support team
Seeks opportunities for continuous learning

ADMINISTRATIVE ASSISTANT II

Responsibilities
Track expenses and develop budget reports using FastCat internal web applications, Excel, and Access
Ensure that all PowerPoint presentations are consistent with FastCat design standards; assist in their production as necessary
Manage records and correspondence, improve systems when necessary; respond to requests for information, maintain office supplies; miscellaneous office tasks as assigned

Requirements
1 to 2 years of office experience with a wide variety of responsibilities
PC proficiency in MS Word, Excel, PowerPoint and electronic calendaring
Well-developed mathematical skills
Comfortable using internet and office software in daily assignments

Competencies
Comfortable working in high-technology environment as part of team
Ability to handle confidential information and perform high quality work
Approaches the work associated with the position professionally
Capable of juggling and prioritizing multiple assignments
Strong budget development/analysis and expense tracking skills; flexibility and commitment
Seeks opportunities for continuous learning

ADMINISTRATIVE LEADER

Responsibilities
Responsible for the smooth operation of all administrative functions
Lead the entire administrative team
Provide leadership to ensure all administrative processes and practices are structured to provide optimal operating effectiveness within the department
Support development and lead implementation and monitoring of internal operating procedures
Initiate discussions about ways to continually improve the smooth functioning of administrative activities and manage projects and objectives associated with process improvement
Make recommendations regarding new technologies and platforms to improve operating systems
Conduct monthly detailed review of budget actual vs. plan, noting exceptions, recommending accruals and following up on tracking exceptions
Create project codes for department activities
Communicate with administrative assistants about the status of individual assignments
Perform administrative duties for FastCat founders such as scheduling meetings, maintaining calendars, completing expense reports, drafting memos, recording and distributing meeting minutes
Become knowledgeable about the work content of the FastCat founders and make daily judgment calls regarding priorities

When required, lead meetings with administrative team to generate ideas, explain new processes and procedures and share pertinent information to support the efficient functioning of the department
Act as an information resource for all administrative team members
Provide assistance to project managers as requested

Requirements
Associate's degree in business administrative studies or related field or five or more years administrative support experience with thorough knowledge of FastCat operations and policies

Competencies
Ability to recognize the need for and then initiate and lead process improvements
Excellent verbal and writing skills as well as interpersonal skills
Resourcefulness
Flexibility/ability to reprioritize quickly
Knowledgeable about business priorities, company organization, people, etc
Approachable/accessible to others
Excellent interpersonal skills

CLIENT ACCOUNT LEADER

Responsibilities
Responsible for all aspects of the relationship with multiple FastCat clients; main responsibility is to ensure clients' satisfaction
Work with FastCat engineering and marketing teams to ensure feasibility and timeliness of new FastCat products
Work with FastCat Project Leaders to ensure that FastCat products meet or exceed customer expectations
Build and maintain good relations with FastCat prospects and customers
Work with clients to produce annual business plans, ensure appropriate approvals both within client company and within FastCat, and ensure clients have full understanding and enthusiasm for plan
Direct all activities related to customer service, training and field support with installing, maintaining, and modifying FastCat products to fit client needs
Generate and present professional proposals to new and existing FastCat customers
Identify client needs and, with assistance of Project Leader, translate needs into software proposals
Follow through on action items obtained from client meetings
Ensure profit margins for all proposals meet targeted margins as established by FastCat
Provide regular, accurate sales forecasts to FastCat executive leadership
Develop policies and procedures for handling contract administration and customer complaints
Liaison with sales and engineering
Lead teams of marketing, sales, and engineering personnel
Coordinate joint sales activities as required

Qualifications
Bachelor's degree; minimum of 8 years of sales experience to business clients
Understanding of medical/health care industry is critical
Complete understanding of FastCat software, its capabilities, and possible extensions

Competencies
Outstanding communication and interpersonal skills
Negotiation and executive-level selling skills
Analytical and creative ability
Ability to coordinate resources
Promote the coordination of efforts among all marketing team members
Approachable/accessible to others

CLINICAL LIAISON

Responsibilities

Use your clinical experience, including your experience with FastCat software, to work with existing customers/clinicians to help them use the software effectively and efficiently in delivering patient care

Develop a working relationship with existing customers such that their clinical practice needs are understood and taken into account in the continuous improvement of FastCat's software

Act as part of a team that demonstrates FastCat software to potential new customers and play a key role in helping them understand how FastCat can help them provide better quality and more effective health care

Provide a clinician's perspective on what potential customers need and how FastCat's software answers those needs in comparison to competing software products

Requirements

At least 5 years clinical experience as a registered nurse, physician assistant, or nurse practitioner

Both inpatient and outpatient experience preferred, but not required

Several years of experience and demonstrated high level expertise in using FastCat software as a clinician

Competencies

Able to effectively demonstrate FastCat software to clinicians

Work well as part of a team

Approachable and accessible to others

Able to interact effectively with health care professionals (eg, nurses, physicians)

GRAPHICS DESIGNER

Responsibilities

Define and implement a unified design vision for interface and Web technologies; produce a variety of design solutions that are consistent with the aesthetic quality, functionality, interface and layout, visual/graphic standards, and look and feel of the FastCat brand

Interact directly with marketing and engineering to achieve buy-in of design vision in order to produce and deliver leading-edge visual and interactive learning elements according to the appropriate requirements and specifications

Seek ways to unify FastCat image through design effort

Create and maintain FastCat web site and promotional materials for both marketing and public relations

Qualifications

Experience in interactive media design and production; navigation design, information design and delivery, interface design

Experience with the integration of design projects with the Web environment

Excellent conceptual, graphic design and typography skills

Experience in optimizing graphics and media for the web

Must be skilled in Photoshop, Illustrator, Flash, HTML, and CSS Experience with audio and video editing software

Experience with high-end animation packages like Alias Wavefront, Maya, Studio Max, Lightwave Proficient with business applications such as MS Office

Bachelor's degree in design (graphics communications, new media design) or related field

Competencies

Being passionate about marrying high technology with fine art

Maintaining professionalism throughout all aspects of the job

Effectively manage multiple projects under tight deadlines with changing priorities

Work well on a creative team in a highly collaborative, fast-paced environment
Ability to focus and listen
Ability to negotiate and be diplomatic
Strong communication and presentation skills
Willing to consider other people's viewpoints

IMPLEMENTATION CONSULTANT

Responsibilities
Responsible for installing and testing software at client work sites
Troubleshoot and resolve any problems that arise following installation
Analyze customer needs and behaviors to use as input into design of features that will enhance usability of applications
Support the daily management and operation of client sites
Keep project leader apprised of progress and milestones
Work with technicians prior to installation to ensure that FastCat software works as designed
Provide accurate information promptly

Requirements
BS degree in Computer Science or related field
At least 3 years experience in software development at FastCat
Proven detailed knowledge of FastCat software
Ability to work with medical personnel, many of whom will be in senior positions in their organization
Ability to translate customer input into improved solutions for common tasks

Competencies
Communicate with team members and clients; support team decisions
Communicate with customers to gather information and fully understand nature of requests
Show respect for all FastCat employees and clients
Represent FastCat in public locations in a professional manner

MARKETING SERVICES REPRESENTATIVE

Responsibilities
Part of marketing team
Responsible for ensuring that client's training needs are met
Develop a communications strategy for a specific FastCat product to improve customer awareness and impact sales
Participate in preparation of marketing presentations
Clarify the terms of the contract with clients as necessary
Provide comprehensive and prompt information for marketing, sales, and engineering professionals
Work with business consultant to assess obligations of proposed contracts

Qualifications
Bachelor's degree in business-related field with aptitude in computers or engineering
Minimum of 3 years in market support work, including product pricing and competitive analysis
Proficiency with MS Office products
Familiar with health/medical care market
Detailed familiarity with FastCat software

Competencies
Familiar with pricing issues and policies
Analytical and detail oriented
Versatile and capable of rapid plan adjustment
Project-oriented
Self-reliant, able to work independently
Good interpersonal skills
Adept at assimilating and prioritizing demands for information from customers and marketing professionals
Actively support marketing team and promote cooperation among members

MARKETING SUPPORT

Responsibilities
Produce, distribute, and log product quotations and revisions requested by marketing services representatives, clients, and product managers
Enter customer leads into database
Distribute appropriate product information
Assist with tracking data for necessary leads/sales forecasting and reporting
Participate in monthly meetings with marketing leaders

Qualifications
BS degree or equal job-related experience
Experience with Microsoft Excel and Word
Some previous sales background or sales-related experience, preferably health/medical care-related

Competencies
Actively support other members of the marketing team
Take personal initiative for sharing information among field representatives and marketing personnel
Detail orientation
Handle multiple tasks and priorities
Seeks opportunities for continuous learning

PROGRAMMER ANALYST

Responsibilities
Using software specifications developed by software developers, create, modify, and test software code
Analyze, debug, and correct code defects identified internally or in the field
Ensure that code and other deliverables adhere to product and company standards
Update and maintain code
Assist in documentation of procedures

Requirements
BS in Engineering or Computer Science or equivalent experience
Knowledge of several of the following areas is desirable: C#, C++, Java Enterprise Edition/AJAX, Microsoft NET, Visual Basic

Competencies
Strong attention to detail
Dependable
Ability to work independently and as part of a team
Ability to meet deadlines
Strong technical ability and logic

PROJECT LEADER

Responsibilities
Ensure that FastCat software meets all technical specifications as developed by Client Account Leader
Lead engineering team including coordinating implementation and client training
Lead client implementations within established schedule and budget
Manage relations with team engineers so that all team members contribute
Responsible for all project communications related to technical issues
Work closely with marketing group to understand client needs
Manage the overall technical development within a project
Provide supervision and direction to software developers/engineers
Open and receptive to new ideas and approaches

Qualifications
Bachelor's or master's degree in Computer Science
Substantial engineering experience with at least one year in management
Knowledge of requirements unique to the health care industry, including privacy legislation compliance
Experience establishing methodologies and processes
Experience implementing projects and leading engineering and information system teams
Well-developed skills in Microsoft Transaction Server (MTS); XML ; Active Server Pages (ASP); Lotus Notes; ERP (Oracle, SAP, PeopleSoft, etc)

Competencies
Resolve issues and break down barriers to effective product implementation
Actively support participation by all team members
Clarify roles and relationships within the team
Develop, recognize, and promote innovative software solutions
Elicit the contribution and professional development of all members of team

PROJECT SUPPORT ASSISTANT

Responsibilities
Support project teams by handling administrative tasks
Track project expenses and time allocations
Keep Project Manager informed in order to keep on schedule and on budget
Interact with FastCat clients to schedule meetings with project members.
These contacts may be of a sensitive, complex, and sometimes confidential nature
Attend such meetings and record minutes as requested
Perform other secretarial and administrative duties for various projects as requested
Provide assistance and back-up responsibilities to other Administrative Assistants
Screen telephone calls and incoming mail
Perform word processing duties; collaborate with various staff and departments in preparing special projects

Requirements
Minimum of high school diploma, with 2 to 4 years in administrative position with wide variety of responsibilities
Knowledgeable about FastCat policies and practices; has access to confidential information
Work requires initiative and independent judgment
Familiar with FastCat software development processes
Proficient in using the internet and with MS Office products, including Word, Excel and PowerPoint

Competencies
Represent FastCat to clients in a professional manner
Comfortable working as part of team in information technology-oriented environment
Broad and detailed knowledge of administrative practices and procedures at FastCat
Strong communications and interpersonal skills
Able to juggle and prioritize wide variety of tasks in a fast-paced work environment
Detail oriented and able to handle confidential information
Dependable and dedicated

QUALITY ASSURANCE ANALYST

Responsibilities
Test FastCat software using various testing strategies such as regression testing, compatibility testing, functional testing, and usability testing prior to release to clients, using both manual and automated testing techniques
Keep accurate records of all testing done and document results; retest after engineers have revised code
Responsible for seeing that problems have been resolved; document resolution
Documentation is an important part of software testing routines at FastCat
Assist with test environment preparation

Qualifications
Associate's degree in Business or Computer Science plus some experience
Understanding of one or more of the following testing tools: Visual Test, SQA, Silk Performer
Experience working with the following databases: SQL Oracle, MS Access
Familiarity with VB, HTM:/DHTML/XML, Active Server Pages, ADO/OLE-DB, IIL (Microsoft Internet Information Server)

Competencies
Strong communication skills
Facilitate team coordination and work effectively as member of team
Ability to accomplish multiple tasks simultaneously
Attention to detail
Able to communicate effectively in technical environment
Willingness to develop an understanding of the marketing requirements for the product

QUALITY ASSURANCE ANALYST A

Responsibilities
Test company product using various testing strategies such as regression testing, compatibility testing, functional testing, stress and volume testing, and testing of release materials using both manual and automated testing techniques
Document errors found and report on project status; verify documentation provided by other team members
Create and revise written procedures to accompany each test method/test applications
Work closely with engineers to devise testing strategies and address issues that arise from testing and special requests

Qualifications
Associate's degree in Business or Computer Science plus at least three years experience in testing environment
Experience working with the following testing tools: Visual Test, SQA, Silk Performer
Experience working with the following databases: SQL Oracle, MS Access
Familiarity with VB, HTM:/DHTML/XML, Active Server Pages, ADO/OLE-DB, IIL (Microsoft Internet Information Server), Active X/COM/DCOM, Java

Competencies
Strong communication skills
Facilitate team coordination and work effectively as member of team
Ability to accomplish multiple tasks simultaneously
Attention to detail
Able to communicate effectively in technical environment
Willing to coach, share expertise with other quality assurance technicians
Willing to ask questions and offer input to engineering staff
Able to adapt to changing priorities and work on several projects at once

SENIOR FELLOW

Responsibilities
Plan and conduct research and development projects of major significance, which are highly difficult and complex in nature, that require expert application of advanced knowledge
Consult with and provide guidance to departments and senior management on complex technical issues set strategy for technical development
Originate and apply new and unique engineering methods and procedures
Review engineers' work and evaluate and coach/develop them
Oversee project managers and serve as resource as needed
Identify new directions for extending products
Provide engineering skills in defining design requirements of product and designing and developing the product
Release design into commercialization

Qualifications
MS/PhD in computer science, business, or related field
Over 8 years experience in all phases of software development, including leading and coaching others
Must have successfully demonstrated cross functional team leadership and have 5+ years supervisory experience of technical personnel
Relevant experience in health care industry

Competencies
Must be cognizant of multiple perspectives and approaches across all engineering projects
Facilitate interaction and exchange among project managers
Work effectively with engineering professionals to ensure the highest quality and reliability of design
Develop strategic product plan
Support marketing and sales efforts through technical support, publishing articles, presentations, key customer visits, and developing key data
Serve as recognized expert within the technical community
Able to develop and utilize global network of professionals to assess technical developments
Demonstrated leadership competencies in a highly technical team
A leader/learner
Often contributes to developments in specialty areas
Serves as behavioral model for engineering group
Approachable/accessible to others
Promotes cooperation and a welcoming environment for all
Anticipates new directions in technology

SENIOR QUALITY ASSURANCE TECHNICIAN

Responsibilities
Responsible for assuring complete performance evaluation of all FastCat web applications through destructive testing
Work closely with software engineers to obtain feedback and offer input to engineering and marketing teams
At the direction of Implementation Consultant, troubleshoot web application installations
Gather, organize, analyze, and summarize data which will lead to improved software analysis
Create and revise written procedures to accompany each test method/test applications
Identify, communicate and provide possible solutions to quality related issues
Maintain organized archive of competitive test results with full traceability to test methods
Train and supervise others on procedures and test methods
Manage the workflow of the quality assurance team
Assist engineers with prioritizing and scheduling quality assurance work

Qualifications
Associate's degree in computer science
A minimum of 5 years in software development and testing
Strong background in statistics and mathematical modeling
Well-developed skills in VB6, HTM:/DHTML/XML, Active Server Pages, ADO/OLE-DB, IIL (Microsoft Internet Information Server), Active X/COM/DCOM, Java; Active Server Pages (ASP); Lotus Notes; ERP (Oracle, SAP, PeopleSoft, etc)
Familiar with C++ programming language
Proficient in the following testing tools: Visual Test, SQA, Silk Performer
Proficient working with the following databases: SQL Oracle, MS Access

Competencies
Good prioritization skills
Able to accomplish multiple assignments simultaneously
Good organizational, written, and communication skills
Attention to detail
Able to create a culture of empowerment that promotes teamwork
Able to recognize and reinforce contribution of members of quality assurance team
Able to stay current with new medical software developments and applications
Able to effectively direct the work of others and ensure accountability of all testing certification
Build working relationships to solve problems and achieve common goals

SOFTWARE ENGINEER

Responsibilities
Design and create engineering specifications for software programs and applications
Work with quality assurance to develop software test plans
Work with hardware engineers to ensure software-hardware compatibility
Analyze FastCat client requirements and translate into technical solutions
Involved in entire project cycle (information gathering, development, deployment, maintenance)
Organize and label data in web sites, intranets, and software to support enhanced usability and access to data
Select appropriate web controls and technologies to design web software in order to give users best possible experience while conforming to legal requirements affecting health care/medical service providers
Extensive collaboration with other development teams

Requirements
Bachelor's degree in computer science or related field
Strong design skills
Excellent verbal/written communication skills
Knowledge of health/medical care systems
Several years' experience with XML, Unix Operating System, Shell, Perl, Solaris, Linux
Ability to work well on teams

Competencies
Excellent communication skills
Meticulous about details
Communicate with engineers/developers in various locations regarding the build process
Create build scripts
Facilitate the prompt and comprehensive sharing of information across engineers/developers
Flexible to new ideas and approaches
Adaptable to changing priorities and demands

SOFTWARE SOLUTIONS CONSULTANT

Responsibilities
Demonstrate FastCat software to potential clients
Performing activities in support of marketing FastCat's product and services
Develop accurate input for client proposals; assist account leaders in preparation of proposals
Assist prospective clients to resolve technical issues by providing liaison with technical and engineering staff
Serve as liaison between engineering and marketing in product development
Maintain a technical understanding of FastCat products
Recognize and promote technical solutions that will be useful to multiple customers
Assist in product positioning and pricing strategies

Qualifications
Bachelor's degree in Business or Computer Science
Minimum 5 years experience in technical sales support, preferably in a medical/health care-related setting
Application software experience
Sales process analysis experience
Management of site survey experience
Technology experience (Microsoft platforms and tools, PC sales tools, Internet)
Complex configuration experience

SOFTWARE USER INTERFACE ARCHITECT

Responsibilities
The engineering face of the company
Responsible for recommending new directions to top engineering leadership
The technical lead on large, complex product implementations for new or existing clients
Research and create the blueprint for the implementation and determine how it will interface with the client's existing applications
Drive innovation by looking beyond customers' articulated needs
Design the system and incorporate it into the client's environment
Implement end-to-end architecture of the system
Ensure that an implementation is built properly and will function to specifications at completion of the implementation

Perform advanced system development, including designing, coding, and testing custom developments as necessary

Consider a range of creative approaches to problems and recommend best-fit solutions that support, extend, and stretch existing products

Communicate requirements to application and database developers for the design and production of software modules and databases as needed in support of new infrastructure and functionality

Conceptualize translations of FastCat software to non-graphics platforms, ie, handheld devices

Supervise software developers as necessary

Provide guidance to rest of technical team

Foster technical and other skill development among engineering staff

Qualifications

Bachelor's degree or masters degree in computer science

Substantial experience designing user interfaces and system integration

Experience as developer or technical lead on software implementation project

Experience working with clients in health care/medical field

Competencies

Problem solving skills - applying technology to solve problems

Developmental skills – able to guide/support/develop other members of the creative team

Creativity – ability to conceive and deliver innovative design

Writing and documentation skills - disciplined and experienced at documenting complex issues

Strong, relevant technical knowledge of Internet/Intranet technologies, client/server, object oriented programming

Excellent communication skills, with ability to lead client meetings and presentations

Consulting experience

Proactive, self-motivated, and able to work effectively with little supervision

Able to communicate technical information to the client, system integrator, and project manager

Able to build consensus around chosen design

Ability to work well on a creative team in a highly collaborative environment

Must be on top of trends and able to keep the company ahead of the curve in software directions

TECHNICIAN

Responsibilities

Coordinate and maintain the error documentation system for FastCat web software

Update files when corrections made

Understand the FastCat software products and company design process

Assist with testing FastCat software using common software testing strategies

Keep accurate records of test results and document results

Perform general support duties such as data entry, routine coding, and miscellaneous project work

Other support duties as assigned

Qualifications

High school diploma or equivalent Proficient in Microsoft PC applications

Strong basic math and computer skills

Familiar with common software testing strategies

Competencies

Good attention to detail

Good prioritization skills

Good verbal and written communication skills

Ability to multitask
Ability to work well with others as well as independently
Ability to maintain a high level of quality
Work effectively as member of a technical team
Seeks opportunities for continuous learning

TRAINING ASSISTANT

Responsibilities
Part of the Client Training Team that trains clients and internal staff to use sophisticated FastCat software
Coordinate, schedule, communicate, and track various tasks for successful implementation of client training initiatives
Coordinate, communicate, and track all client training events and activities
Maintain Microsoft Access database of client training records
Develop and run queries and reports on training progress
Maintain the Client Training Team website and associated materials
At the direction of Client Training Manager and Client Account Leaders, communicate with media designers to ensure on-time development of appropriate training materials
Schedule multiple training rooms, and communicate with internal clients and facilities to meet demand for training space
Be knowledgeable of all client training processes and procedures and be willing to establish tools/templates to support the processes
Suggest process improvements
Implement tasks that support the established or new processes
Support the Client Training Manager and staff as determined by needs of the business
High proficiency with MS Office software (ie Excel, Word, Powerpoint, Access, Visio)

Qualifications
Minimum 4 year Bachelor's Degree or equivalent
Minimum 1–2 years of experience in an administrative or customer service role
1-2 years experience health/medical care-related experience helpful (nursing or related occupation)

Competencies
Able to respond quickly and professionally to rapidly changing business culture
Excellent written, verbal, presentation, and facilitation skills
Strong analytical, logical, and organizational skills combined with an acute attention-to-detail
Ability to successfully manage multiple priorities and be a self-starter
Customer focused
Basic knowledge of HTML, web authoring tools, or knowledge management systems

TRAVEL COORDINATOR

Responsibilities
Responsible for booking all aspects of future travel (flights, hotels, car rental) including receiving initial and change trip requests via email, phone, or fax
Ensure that travel needs are met within the constraints of FastCat's travel budget
Complete all pertinent trip details, provide timely itineraries, perform follow-up and liaison for other traveler-identified needs
Communicate with FastCat travelers regarding their preferences for flight schedules, airlines, hotel
Work with FastCat preferred vendors with ensure best rates on all aspects of travel

Document communications with FastCat employees and vendors
Be familiar with and assist travelers to obtain any required documentation such as pass-ports or visas
Maintain travel budgets
Ensure travel charged to proper project budget
Keep project managers and others informed as to travel budget status

Requirements
Absolute attention to detail
Detail-oriented
A high level of accuracy is required in performing duties according to pre-existing guidelines
Thorough knowledge of Excel Comfortable working with web applications and use of internet
Able to communicate accurately and professionally with FastCat employees and vendors
Familiar with FastCat guidelines on travel budgets
High school diploma with 1-2 years office experience, preferably within FastCat

Competencies
Exercise tact when dealing with FastCat employees
Demonstrate good listening skills
Able to communicate effectively both within and outside FastCat
Ability to work with a team
Enthusiasm for travel

USER INTERFACE DESIGNER

Responsibilities
Visualize projects from viewpoint of end users
Work with clients to extract web design that will best suit their needs
Facilitate design process with clients and marketing team to resolve areas of indecisiveness
Suggest optimal design solutions
Focus on content development, usability, and interaction design on multiple, simultaneous projects
Design specifications for and perform programming and testing activities on a new or existing large client implementation
Participate in design meetings for related projects as requested
Develop estimates for identified tasks
Perform development activities per estimates (can include coding or scripting)
Assign tasks in site production, image preparation, and data management
Review curriculum developed by Client Training team for end users
Assess training materials for usability and completeness

Requirements
Bachelor's degree in Computer Science; substantial programming experience
Understand the entire development process, including specifications, documentation and quality assurance
Outstanding technical knowledge in software development methodologies, design, and implementation
Must have solid practices for unit testing and documentation of developed code

Competencies
Strong interpersonal skills
Communicate effectively with other software developers and architects, marketing team, and Client Training team

Proactive self-motivator who can work effectively with little supervision
Able to help teams achieve their quality and schedule goals
Receptive to new ideas and approaches
Works to understand alternative perspectives
Demonstrates innovation and creativity

VISIONARY CHAMPION

Responsibilities
Research and recommend features and expanded medical/health care market segments to pursue
Define and ensure the success of new features/functions and planning overall strategy
Guide product direction to FastCat marketing group
Define key customer needs (ones they know about and ones that have not yet surfaced)
Identify market and technological drivers
Stay current (and ahead of the crowd) on new technological innovations that can be leveraged to shape the market and product
Iterate with product development to ensure product specifications are consistent with market requirements
Articulate the opportunity for the features/functions, clarify tradeoffs between opportunities
Prioritize feature development and provide technological input to the product roadmap
Provide business and market leadership to the cross-functional team that develops and delivers the product
Identify, drive and deliver content, material and tools for training marketing team
Work with marketing to ensure materials ready for launch
Ensure key messages align with strategy
Establish and manage revenue objectives for new and existing products including competitive analysis

Experience
Bachelor's degree in technical area, plus MBA or equivalent
5+ years of related experience with previous management experience in a technical field
Familiarity with all aspects of medical/health care market is essential

Competencies
Establish, implement, and maintain quality service standards that assure maximum customer satisfaction
Understand key customer needs and medical market segments
Promote cooperation and team orientation among product managers
Mentor development of product managers
Fashion innovative solutions that promote quality thinking across FastCat marketing
Organized, motivated, self-directed, sound business judgment
Ability to ensure that everyone's contribution to the team is fully recognized and utilized
Approachable/accessible to all

PHASE II EXTERNAL COMPETITIVENESS:

Pricing the Structure

In Phase II you will analyze external market survey data on total compensation and price your structure. Market data lets you analyze the forms of pay used by competitors and attach dollars to the internal structure you recommended in Phase I. Additionally, you will integrate pressures from inside FastCat (Internal Alignment) and outside (External Competitiveness) through the use of grades and ranges or bands and zones.

Specially written software will help with your Phase II analysis. Software directions are on the next two pages.

A road map for your work in Phase II follows.

DIRECTIONS FOR USING THE *CASES ACCESS* (SOFTWARE) *FILES*

Two Access files accompany *Cases in Compensation*. Access is part of Microsoft Office software. You do not need to know how to use Access before you use the *Cases* Access files. However, **Access must be installed on the computer or network you will be using.** To use the *Cases* Access files, **save a copy of them to a non-network, non-shared drive such as your hard drive or a flash drive**.

About Access Software

Access is database management software that helps you examine information in an organized fashion. **Data entry forms** let you enter and edit data. **Reports** allow you to view and print the results of the data you entered. The Phase II software contains seven data entry and four "View and Print" forms.

To Obtain the *Cases* Access Database Files From a Network or Course Website

Your school may give you specific instructions for locating the software on the school's network (and setting a password for your team) or course website. If you have not been given any special instructions, follow these.

(1) Open the Microsoft Access software program from the Windows Start menu. (In some cases, Access will be found under "Microsoft Office" on the Start menu.)

(2) From the main Access menu, choose **File**. Then choose **Open**. Locate the folder that contains the Access database file (having an .mdb extension) for Phase II. Highlight the file name you wish to open and (again) click **Open**. There will either be one version of the file that all groups will copy for their own use or there will be multiple versions of the file, one for each group. (If the latter, the files may have names that correspond to each group/team, such as "TeamA_PhaseII.mdb.") If there is one version of the file, either on a network drive or on a course website, you will typically want to copy it to a hard drive or flash drive and then begin your work on Phase II. You can also copy the file to your hard drive or flash drive if there is already a file earmarked for your group's use. If, however, you intend to work from a network drive that has shared access, you will want to make your own unique copy (if not already created for you) of the .mdb Access database file. Assign it a unique name and also assign a password to the file. (See below.)

(3) If you wish to assign a password to your copy of the file, do the following steps **in order**. From the main Access menu, choose **File**. Then choose **Open**. Highlight the file name you wish to open. Do **not**, however, click on **Open** yet. Instead, click on the downward facing arrow next to Open. Then, click on **Open Exclusive**.

(4) After you have opened the Access database file using **Open Exclusive** and you see the "**Phase II Session Login Screen**," click on the "**Set Password**" button and enter a password that everyone on your team will remember. In future sessions, you can open the software simply by double clicking on the name of the file. You will not need to open Access first. However, **you will need to enter your password to open the file.**

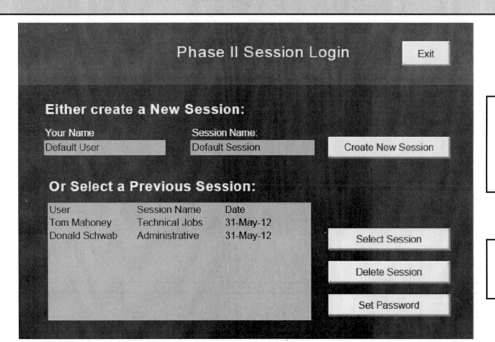

To Use the *Cases* Access (.mdb) Files (on Your Own Computer)

Use Windows Explorer to locate the drive and folder in which the software is located. Find the "**Phase.II.11e.mdb**" file. Then open it by double clicking on it. As noted above, save and work with the file from a non-network drive such as your hard drive or flash drive.

Session Login

Enter your team's name and a session name. Use the buttons on the right column to "**Create New Session**" or to resume work on a previous session — "**Select Session**". You will be able to create multiple sessions by giving each one a different name. Multiple sessions will permit you to compare the results of different analyses.

The *Cases* software automatically saves information when you change to a new form or exit (if working from a non-network, non-shared drive). However, the software only does the mathematical calculations when you go to the REGRESSION screen. So if you go back and change any data, be sure to go to the REGRESSION screen so that the software updates the calculations.

To see this saved information, reopen the software (remember your password if you assigned one) and select the right session.

MAIN MENU has 3 parts: *Session Information, Select Data*, and *View or Print.*

Session Information

Identifies the user and the title of this session.

Select Data

The first time you use the software, **you must** enter information on the "Select Data" forms **in the order** in which they are listed on the Main Menu. For example, you should not attempt to complete the 'Companies' step unless you have already completed 'Benchmark Jobs' and 'Match with FastCat Jobs.'

View and Print

Here you can view the results of your "Select Data" decisions, as well as print and/or export results.

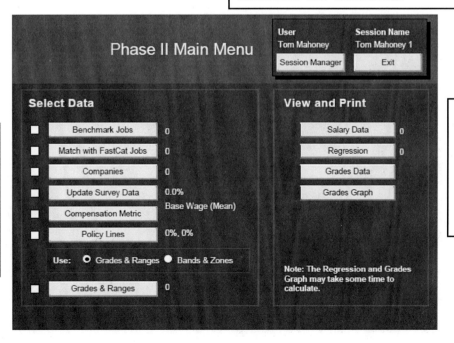

PHASE II (External Competitiveness) STEPS

Step 1: Recommend Strategy for Competitiveness

What are alternatives? What's best for FastCat?

What pay level?

What mix of forms?

How to integrate internal and external structure?

Does strategy support objectives?

Consistent with previous strategic decisions?

Step 2: Design Survey

Relevant market?

Job matches?

Forms of pay?

Age the data?

Compensation metric?

Good fit?

Step 3: Choose Pay Policy Line

On which pay forms?

Consistent with strategy?

For which jobs/grades/bands?

Step 4: Integrate Internal & External Structure

Grades/ranges or bands/zones?

Natural breaks in work flow?

Does overlap facilitate career paths?

Tradeoff: flexibility *vs.* guidelines

Step 5: Evaluate Your Decisions

And finally: <u>Write Your Report</u>

BACKGROUND

The result of your work in Phase I was a structure (or perhaps more than one structure) for FastCat to help achieve the compensation objectives you recommended. In Phase II, you will further develop FastCat's strategy by recommending how much, and how, you want to pay FastCat employees relative to how much and how Fast-Cat competitors pay their employees—external competitiveness. The discussion of markets, competitors, and employees' behavior in the *Compensation* textbook, particularly Chapters 7 and 8, provides background for these issues.

Compensation comes in several forms: base, bonus, long-term incentives (stock) and benefits. ***What forms*** of pay should be included in your analysis of what FastCat competitors are paying? What mix of forms should FastCat include in its own pay plan? ***How much*** to pay will depend on how you define FastCat competitors and measure the market. The software, described earlier, helps you analyze both how and how much FastCat competitors pay for jobs similar to those at FastCat.

You should also recognize the tradeoffs required to ***integrate pressures from outside and inside FastCat***. For example, the structure that exists in the external market—the pay levels and differentials between jobs at Fast-Cat competitors—may not correspond to the internal structure you recommended for FastCat. Some FastCat jobs that appear to be similar to those in the external market may be worth more (or less) to FastCat than they are in the external market. The use of grades and ranges or bands and zones will help you reconcile these differences.

In sum, there are three things to focus on:

(1) ***What forms*** of pay competitors are using (pay mix);

(2) ***How much*** competitors are paying (pay level); and

(3) ***External structure:*** how one job is paid compared to another by FastCat competitors, and how the external pay structure compares to FastCat's internal structure.

Caution

Do not wait for your instructor to complete classroom discussion of the related chapters in the book before you begin Phase II. If you do, you will not have enough time to complete the assignment. Also, do not jump right to the software. Rather, start by skimming the entire Phase II section of this casebook and Chapters 7 and 8 in the *Compensation* textbook. Get an overall picture of what needs to be done. Make some preliminary decisions. Then look at the software to see how it can help you do it.

STEP 1: RECOMMEND A STRATEGY ON EXTERNAL COMPETITIVENESS

This is the third part of your overall compensation strategy (objectives, alignment, ***competitiveness***, performance, and management). It includes three aspects: pay level (how much), mix of pay forms (what: relative importance of each pay form), and how to integrate internal and external pay structures.

Pay Level

FastCat's pay level is the sum of the wages for all employees divided by the number of employees. A separate pay level can be calculated for each job family, e.g., sum of wages for all engineers divided by number of engineers. However, pay level generally refers to the average for the entire company. Usually, pay level is first calculated using base pay. Then other pay forms are considered.

How should the pay level at FastCat compare to that of its competitors? Should FastCat lead (pay more than) its competitors in the external market, pay at the market (match competitors), or lag (pay less than) the market?

Should FastCat have a different pay level policy for different types of work (i.e., pay above the market for engineers and match the market for administrative work)? Your choice has implications for FastCat's labor costs and ability to attract and retain talent. Remember that any choice you make faces some problems. Anticipate the problems created by either a uniform or a differentiated market policy and tell how you hope to minimize them.

Mix of Forms

Chapter One of the textbook defines compensation as "all forms of financial returns and tangible services and benefits." Which forms should FastCat emphasize? Strategically, you could differentiate FastCat from its competitors by its pay mix rather than by pay level. For example, FastCat may choose to lag its competitors in base pay but have bonuses sufficiently large that its *total compensation* meets the market. Its emphasis on various pay forms may differ from its competitors. *How much* (total compensation) will match, but *what* (mix) will differ. In good years (when FastCat is *really* a fast cat), its *total compensation* may even lead its competitors.

How to decide on a pay level and mix strategy? Go back to FastCat's business strategy. What is FastCat trying to accomplish, and what level and mix will be most helpful to do that? For example, would FastCat gain a competitive advantage by using bonuses on top of base pay that already matches competitors' rates? Or will this strategy only add to labor costs? Perhaps a better approach might be to lag the market and hope that the opportunity to work on exciting projects will attract, retain, and motivate? What difference will your choices make?

Integrate the External and Internal Structure

The third part of the external competitive strategy concerns how to integrate FastCat internal structure that you designed in Phase I with the structure that exists in the external market. Generally this is done through the use of either grades and ranges or bands and zones.

Preliminary Ideas

Because you do not have enough information to recommend a competitive policy strategy yet, make some preliminary judgments based on what you have read in the *Compensation* textbook. Use these to provide initial direction. They can be revised once you better understand the external market data. Rethink your strategy recommendations throughout your work on Phase II. Remember that strategies can change as a result of more information.

STEP 2: DESIGN A SURVEY OF TOTAL COMPENSATION AT FASTCAT'S COMPETITORS

The software contains pay information for over 28,000 employees in 27 jobs in 60 companies. You will choose which companies, jobs, and compensation metrics to use in a survey for FastCat. The software then organizes the data and does the mathematical calculations. The software categorizes pay forms as *base, short-term* and *long-term incentives,* and *benefits.*

Base wage is the cash amount an employer and employee agree to as a condition of employment. Base wages in the survey range from under $20,900 paid to an entry-level Technician to over $230,300 paid to a Marketing Manager 3.

Incentives are tied directly to a performance target specified ahead of time. The performance target can be set for individual employees, a team, a business unit, or the entire organization. If the target is met, the incentive is paid. Incentives do not affect base pay. FastCat does not have any incentive plans.

Short-term incentives or bonuses are paid in cash, and are usually calculated on a time interval of one year or less. Eighty-one percent of the employees included in the survey (included in the software) receive some form of short-term incentive.

Long-term incentives typically take the form of stock options or stock grants. Thus, their value is based on changes in the price of the company's stock. Thirty-eight percent of the employees in the software database receive any long-term incentives.

Benefits include time away from work, services, and retirement/protection. (Legally required benefits are not included in the survey.) FastCat has always considered its benefits standard for the area and industry. But it has never done any analysis of what its competitors offer. FastCat has not asked employees how they feel about their benefits, nor has anyone paid much attention to their costs or the value received from those costs.

Keep in mind that you are NOT designing any kind of variable pay or benefits plan as part of Phase II. Instead, you are analyzing the use of these pay forms among FastCat competitors and recommending a *strategy* for using them in FastCat's total compensation plan.

Designing a survey includes a number of steps:

A.	Select benchmarks and match survey jobs with FastCat jobs
B.	Select competitors in FastCat's relevant external market
C.	Analyze the data:
		Adjust the survey data to account for its age
		Decide which pay forms to compare
		Decide which compensation metric to use
D.	Be sure you understand your statistical results
E.	Evaluate the 'fit" between FastCat and its market.

BEFORE YOU GO TO THE COMPUTER, READ ALL PHASE II INSTRUCTIONS

Look over the descriptions of the jobs included in the database **(Appendix A)** and the companies in the database **(Appendix B)** and decide which of these match FastCat. Read the definitions of the various compensation metrics **(Exhibits 17 and 18)** and decide what analysis will be useful before you do it. ***Don't use the software to substitute for thinking.*** Always be sure you know WHY you are making decisions. Emphasize that "why" in your written report.

A. Select Benchmarks and Match with FastCat Jobs

Compare the descriptions of the jobs included in the software **(Appendix A)** with the FastCat jobs from Phase I. Decide which jobs match. These will be the ones to include in your analysis.

How many matches?

Try to match at least three jobs in each structure (if you have multiple structures)—one at the bottom, one at the top, and one in the middle. The more structures you used in Phase I, the more benchmark jobs you will need to adequately price the structure.

The more benchmark jobs you find, the more confidence you will have in your results—*IF your matches are strong*. On the other hand, mismatches mean faulty decisions, which will affect costs, turnover, and FastCat's ability to attract/retain the people it needs.

Exhibit 16 Matching Jobs

FASTCAT JOB	POINT VALUE	JOB MATCH FROM SURVEY
Admin aide	25	Office Support 1
Technician	50	Technician 1
Travel coordinator	75	Office Support 2
Green guru	100	Office Support 5

If you cannot find sufficient matches, keep notes on the "goodness" of the nearest match (i.e., *"survey job x has more (less) responsibility than the closest FastCat job x"*). This information will be useful when you integrate the FastCat structure with market rates. For each survey job you match, record the JE points you assigned to the FastCat job in Phase I. Include a chart showing the matches and the JE points, as in **Exhibit 16**. Consider also using benchmark conversion/leveling, which is described in *Compensation*.

*If your plan does not include points...*you still need a way to price the structure. One way is to take jobs at the bottom and top of your structure and identify survey jobs that match the closest. These become your links to the external market. For example, if you have a single structure for all FastCat jobs and do not have points, you can take your lowest job, say Administrative Aide, and try to match it with a survey job. Does the job description for Administrative Aide match the Office Support I job in the survey? Or does it better match Office Support II, or Office Support III? You decide. Then do the same at the top of your structure, with, say, the Senior Fellow job. Does the Senior Fellow match the Engineering Manager I, II, or III? The more parts of your structure that you can match well in the market, the more information you will have to guide your decisions.

Use the software to select the survey jobs and then continue with steps B and C below. Prior to conducting a regression analysis, go to the *Salary Data: Summary Report* part of the software to see the market rates for your survey benchmarks. Then draw a graph by hand with $ on the vertical axis. Put your lowest-level job as the first point on the horizontal axis and your highest-level job at the far right end of your horizontal axis. Find the $ (from survey data) for each of the jobs on your graph (vertical axis), and draw a line connecting the points. This will be your market line. Slot in the other jobs in this structure between the highest and lowest point. Draw your grades and ranges/bands and zones by hand.

B. Select Competitors in FastCat's External Market

Sixty companies in FastCat's geographical area are included in the software. **Appendix B** provides the following information on these companies: size (less than 400 employees-small, between 400 and 1,000 employees-medium, over 1,000 employees-large); industry (computers and hardware; semiconductors; software; financial; manufacturing); a brief description; and information on its forms of pay.

You may want to look at different companies for different purposes. For example, you may decide that all companies in a single industry provide the best match for setting base wages. Or, you may want to look at only those companies that offer long-term incentives. Or, look at all 60 companies. The software makes multiple comparisons easy. Run several comparisons to see what difference company selection makes.

Be sure to discuss your comparisons and conclusions based on them in your report. Your boss will have more confidence in your recommendations if you back them up with thorough analysis.

Remember that your selection of companies should be based on business and work-related logic. Be sure to include that logic in your report, along with a list of the companies you selected. Did the selection of companies make any difference?

As you examine the survey data, you will see that *no single rate exists for a job.* Rather, a distribution of pay rates exists. The rates you attach to your structure will depend on how you define the relevant market for FastCat, i.e., which jobs, pay forms, and companies you include in your analysis.

At the Computer....

Read the directions for using the software. They provide the "how-to." This section provides the "why" for the first three data entry forms used in the Phase II software. As noted previously, the first time you go through the following **steps**, do them **in order**.

BENCHMARK JOBS

Choose which of the 27 survey jobs to include in your analysis. (Scroll down to see all 27 jobs.) Jobs can either be selected individually by checking the box, or you can use the "Select All" button. "More info" will allow you to read the description of the survey job.

NOTE: At least three jobs must be selected for the regression analysis to work properly.

MATCH WITH FASTCAT JOBS

For each survey job included, enter the title of the matching FastCat job and the JE points you assigned that job in Phase I. Not all the survey jobs will match FastCat jobs.

COMPANIES

Look at the "More Info" for each of the 60 companies. Then choose which companies you wish to include in your analysis.

After you have made your choices on jobs and companies, look at the reports described below

REPORTS USED

SALARY DATA

Shows actual salary data included in your analysis. Before you press this button, notice the summary to the right of the button. This figure tells you how many individual employee salaries are included in your analysis.

You have choices in Salary Data, either a summary report, a detail report, or both.

Summary Report

For each benchmark job you selected, the summary report provides the number of individuals in that job in the companies you selected, and the base salary, total cash, and total compensation for that job. The report also includes the mean, weighted mean, and quartiles for base salary, total cash, and total compensation.

Detail Report

The detail report provides the base wage, bonuses, stock options, and benefits paid to every individual in the benchmark job among the companies you selected.

Use the scroll bar on the side to move around a single page; use the arrow bar on the bottom of the window to move back and forth among pages. Use the icon bar at the top of the screen to print the report or to change the way it is displayed in the window.

C. Analyze the Data:

(1) Adjust the survey data to account for its age

It takes time to collect and analyze salary survey data. By the time you receive it, the survey data are already six months old. Since you are designing a pay system for a future period, the data must be projected into the future. What percentage will you use to update the data? Justify your update percentage in your report.

> **Ask Your Instructor**
>
> *Your instructor may provide an estimate of how much the market has been moving in the past.* Specify the percent you will use to update or "age" the data.

(2) Decide what forms of pay to compare

You can use any of three compensation measures for your market line: base, total cash (base + short-term incentives), or total compensation (base + benefits + short-term and long-term incentives). Trying out more than one measure and comparing results will give you a fuller **picture** of the external market.

Start with base wage as a guide for setting pay rates but look at total cash or total compensation for assessing FastCat's overall competitiveness. Choosing only those companies that offer long-term incentives and then comparing their total cash versus their total compensation would provide information to guide a recommendation on long-term incentives at FastCat. Similar comparisons can be made on short-term incentives, which you will be working in Phase III. **Exhibit 17** considers what these different comparisons will tell you.

Exhibit 17 Compensation Metrics

FORMS	USEFULNESS	LIMITATION
Base	Tells how competitors are valuing the work in similar jobs	Fails to include performance incentives and other forms, so will not give true picture if competitors offer low base but high incentives
Total Cash (Base + Bonus)	Tells how competitors are valuing work; also tells the cash pay for performance opportunity in the job	All employees may not receive incentives, so it may overstate the competitors' pay; plus, it does not include long-term incentives
Total Compensation (Base + Bonus + Profit Sharing + Benefits)	Tells the total value competitors place on this work	All employees may not receive all the forms. Be careful; don't set FastCat base equal to competitors' total compensation. Risks high fixed costs at FastCat

(3) Choose a metric

You can choose among a variety of measures for your analysis, depending on which pay forms you are focusing on. For base wage and total cash, there are four different metrics: mean, 25th percentile, 50th percentile, and 75th percentile. For total compensation, there is an additional metric: weighted mean. **Exhibit 18** defines these metrics.

Exhibit 18 Definitions of Compensation Metrics

> **Mean:** The total value of all rates reported for each job, divided by the number of employees at that company in that job. There is one mean per job per company.
>
> **Quartiles:** Data is arranged from lowest to highest. Quartiles locate the data that fall at the 25th, 50th, and 75th percentiles.
>
> **Weighted Mean**: Each company's mean is weighted by the number of people in that company in that job.

Which metric is the best measure of "average pay" in your relevant labor market? Try several to see what difference it makes. For example, does using the mean dilute the influence of very large companies? Once again, use results from your analysis of various options to support your recommendations.

D. Be Sure You Understand your Results

The software uses regression analysis to generate a market line.

What is a regression line?

Pay rates in the market (competitors) are regressed on job evaluation points to draw a straight line that summarizes the market rates for benchmark jobs. **Exhibit 19** shows the regression that resulted when all jobs were selected, with each job receiving 10 JE points more than the previous job. (This analysis was done to help you understand regression. It does not illustrate sound compensation decisions.)

Exhibit 19 shows the FastCat structure (as measured by job evaluation points) on the x (horizontal) axis; pay rates for each benchmark job are on the y (vertical) axis. The diamonds are the jobs, located on the graph according to the JE points for the matching FastCat job (x axis) and the pay rate for the survey job. You could draw a line freehand to connect the actual data points (the diamonds) and use that for a market line. Or, you can use the software to calculate a "least squares" regression. Regression finds the straight line that minimizes the squared distance between all the points and the line. This will be the "market line" for your survey.

Exhibit 19 Regression Results

NOTE: You can export your graphs to a clipboard and from there into another program by using the button on this page.

Equation is the regression line (y = ax +b) solved for this analysis.

The **R²** is a measure of fit between the market data and the JE points you assigned the FastCat jobs in Phase 1.

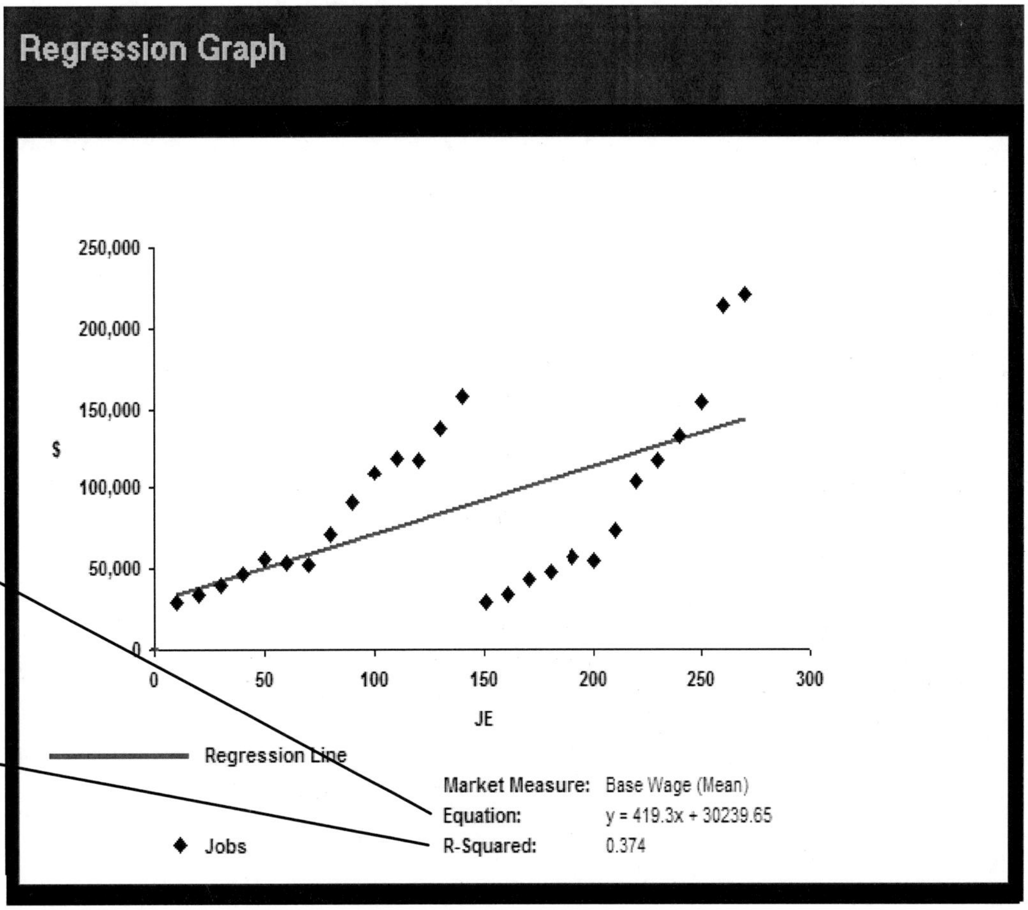

Market Measure: Base Wage (Mean)
Equation: $y = 419.3x + 30239.65$
R-Squared: 0.374

NOTE: Be sure that you use the Regression command when you have completed this first set of decisions. If you decide to go back and change your selection of companies or job matches, be sure to use the Regression command again. The Regression command has the effect of telling the software to "do the calculation."

Do multiple analyses to better understand the market

Exhibit 20 describes the mathematical relationship between this straight line and your survey data. Going through the logic in the exhibit will help you understand the results of your analysis. Spend some time studying the graph of your regression and your data to understand your results before you go on to the rest of Phase II. For example, we already noted that **Exhibit 19** was constructed using every single survey job and giving each one 10 more JE points than the previous one. The pattern of the diamonds suggests at least three groupings, maybe more. These groups may constitute separate markets for each job family.

You may find it useful to run separate trials on different job families, e.g., only engineering jobs, or only marketing jobs. Or, if in your results, some of the jobs cluster away from your market line, run a separate analysis of only those jobs. All of these comparisons will give you a better feel for what is going on in the external market.

Exhibit 20 Do the Math

The formula for a line is $y = a + bx$, where

  y = Predicted Salary, i.e., what the regression predicts will be the wage for a job of x points
  x = Job Evaluation Points
  a = the place where the line crosses the y axis; where $x = 0$
  b = slope of the line; in this case, the dollar value of each additional JE point

Regression analysis estimates the values for a and b that best fit the data you included in your analysis.

The market line in Exhibit 19 is $y = 419.3(x) + 30239.65$, which means that a FastCat job is predicted to receive a wage of $30239.65 plus an additional $419.30 for each job evaluation point. A job with 80 points would receive $30239.65 + ($419.30 * 80) = $63783.65 a month. (The symbol * means multiply.)

Using your values for a and b, construct a table similar to the one below for all FastCat jobs, including non-benchmark jobs.

Job	JE Points	Salary Measure: Base wage, Mean
Technician	20	$39,626
Office Leader	30	$42,818
Software Solutions Consultant	80	$63,784

E. Evaluate the "Fit" between FastCat and the Market

The software also calculates a statistic that describes the "goodness" of the fit between your FastCat structure and the structure (i.e., pay relationships among jobs) in the external market, R-squared (also referred to as R^2), is a measure of the degree of relationship between variables. Salary (base, cash compensation, or total compensation) is the dependent variable, and job evaluation points are the independent variable that "explains" or is associated with the variation in salary. The higher the R^2, the more salary is associated with job evaluation points.

What Does the R^2 Mean?

R^2 ranges from .00 to 1.00. The higher the R^2, the more similar is the FastCat structure to what its competitors use (as measured by the survey you designed). A low R^2, as in **Exhibit 19** ($R^2 = 0.374$) is obtained to the degree that benchmark jobs are distant from the market line.

A low R^2 may mean that FastCat has a genuine difference with its competitors over the relative value of some job(s). If you get a low R^2, you must decide whether you are going to go with the market (price the job according to the market rate) or the internal results (price the job more according to the internal consistency such as FastCat unique workflows). Do you change your Phase I structure to match (mimic?) your competitors' decisions (as reflected in the market)? Or do you stick with your Phase I recommendations? Recall that being "strategic" includes differentiating yourself from competitors. But what are the negative consequences of either position? Be strategic, but do not simply overpay or underpay relative to competitors. How do you balance the two extremes? How will you gain acceptance of the leadership and employees for your recommendation?

Judging Acceptable Results

What is an acceptable R^2? That depends on what FastCat wants to accomplish. Keep in mind that this project is NOT about getting an R^2 of 1.00. This project is about designing the right pay structure for FastCat.

What you are doing when you examine R^2 is considering the fit between FastCat's job structure and the external compensation structure: integrating internal and external pressures. How tightly do you wish FastCat's structure to reflect its competitors' job structure? Can you defend your recommendations in terms of how they align with FastCat business strategy and objectives? Be sure to address the issue of goodness of fit in your report.

Before you go on, spend some time thinking about your results thus far.

Take a Break

IF YOU DON'T UNDERSTAND YOUR RESULTS...

Print your decisions and results from the software program, rethink and reread.

IF YOU AREN'T SATISFIED WITH YOUR RESULTS...

Print one set of results, then revise your decisions by entering new information. Print those results, then spend some time comparing and thinking. Try any number of revisions until you feel comfortable with what you are doing.

IF YOU THINK YOUR RESULTS ARE DYNAMITE...

We still encourage you to print your results and come back later. The next step in Phase II is to integrate internal FastCat pressures and external market pressures. What you do here will be crucial to the success of your plan at FastCat. This step will be much easier to do and will be more successful if you have spent some time understanding your Phase II results thus far, thought about how they fit with Phase I, and have a sense of what kinds of grades and ranges (or bands and zones) can help FastCat. When you are ready to go on....

At the Computer....

UPDATE SURVEY DATA

Enter the percentage to update the base wages to project the existing data into a future time frame. NOTE: While the survey contains data on base wages, benefits, short-term incentives, and long-term incentives, only the base wages will be updated.

COMPENSATION METRIC

Select the metric that you want to use for your particular analysis.
Spend some time looking at this REPORT:

REGRESSION

Displays a graph of the straight line that best fits your data points (JE points for FastCat matching jobs). A statistical calculation of the straight line that best fits these jobs and their associated salary data. Use the button to export the resulting graph for use in another program if you wish.

STEP 3: CHOOSE PAY POLICY LINE

The market line illustrates the "going rate" paid by competitors in your labor market. If you wish to lead or lag the market, create a policy line reflecting the external competitiveness policy you specified in STEP 1. The software lets you set two different policy lines, and then choose which one applies to each grade (or band). So for each grade (or band), you can either use the market line or one of the two policy lines you specify. Specify your policy lines for each grade and tell why you are making this recommendation. What will it do for FastCat?

STEP 4: INTEGRATE INTERNAL AND EXTERNAL STRUCTURES

The pay policy line addressed FastCat's pay for **benchmark** (key) jobs relative to the external market.

The next step is to slot in the rest of FastCat's jobs. As you do so, you will be integrating FastCat's internal structure and external competitors' structure. Merging will be easier if there is flexibility in your system.

Three options exist for introducing flexibility into the balancing process:

- Use a separate flat rate for each job;
- Group jobs into grades and establish a pay range for each grade; and
- Use bands and zones to combine employees in different types of work into the same general level.

Because grades/ranges and bands/zones permit the integration of internal alignment and external competitiveness, this is a major part of the Phase II assignment. You will want to spend a lot of time thinking about, adjusting, and fine-tuning your decisions on exactly where to divide your grades (or bands) and what size ranges (or zones) to use. The software lets you easily switch between entering/revising data on the "Select Data" forms and seeing those results on the data reports.

Flat Rates

If you believe it supports FastCat's objectives, you could design a flat rate for each job or skill level: all employees in a job (or skill/competency level) are paid the same rate regardless of experience, performance, etc. Flat rates are common in skill-based plans and frequently specified in union contracts. Use the statistics described in **Exhibit 20** "Do the Math" to calculate flat rates.

Exhibit 21 Flat Rates

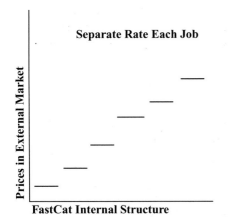

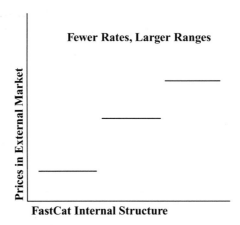

Exhibit 21 illustrates two options for constructing pay structures with flat rates. A separate rate for every job, with narrow differentials between jobs (sketch on left) allows more promotions. But a second option is fewer rates with wider differentials between them (sketch on right). If you decide on fewer flat rates, you would group your jobs into grades (see **Exhibit 22**) and then set a single rate for the entire grade.

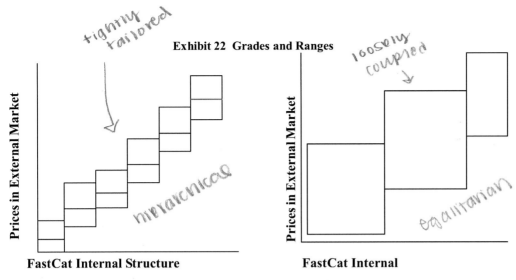

tightly tailored

loosely coupled

Exhibit 22 Grades and Ranges

hierarchical

egalitarian

Prices in External Market

FastCat Internal Structure

Prices in External Market

FastCat Internal

Grades and Ranges

Grades refer to a distance along the x axis, i.e., a division of job evaluation results (see **Exhibit 22**). Ranges refer to a distance along the y axis, i.e., dollar amounts that set the minimum and maximum pay permissible for a job within a grade. Grouping jobs into grades and establishing a pay range for each grade makes a system easier to administer. All jobs that fall within a grade are treated the same for compensation purposes.

How Many Grades and Ranges?

In order to design grades and ranges that make sense for FastCat, review the job structure you constructed in Phase I. Natural breaks in the job structure and the nature of the organization structure should help you determine how many grades to use and which jobs should be in which grades. Wider and fewer grades with larger pay ranges (on the right in **Exhibit 22**) are consistent with a more flexible organization structure. Narrower grades (left; **Exhibit 22**) allow more frequent promotions. *Remember that any jobs that you assign to the same grade will be treated as if they are of equal worth to FastCat.*

What Size Ranges?

Ranges have midpoints, minimums and maximums. Also important is the concept of **Range Spread**, defined as (Salary Range Maximum-Salary Range Minimum)/Salary Range Minimum. **Exhibit 23** shows typical salary range spreads as a function of pay structure type (market-based is most common with a typical range spread of 47 % to 58 %) and job level (larger spreads at higher job levels).

Exhibit 23 Grade Range Spread Practices by Pay Structure Type and Job Level

Pay Structure Type	Range Spread
Traditional (N = 139)	36 % to 46 %
Market-based (N = 443)	47 % to 58 %
Broadbands (N = 66)	85 % to 153 %

Job Level (N = 561 to 645)	Range Spread
Hourly	43%
Salaried, except Executive	55%
Executive	65%

range that you give mgmt to determine pay for their ppl flexible

Source: Figures 25a, 25b, 25c, "Compensation Programs and Practices 2012," WorldatWork, October 2012. Job level range spreads are medians computed from the source figures.

N is the number of organization respondents.

Range spread = (max - min)/min = max/min – 1.

Midpoints

The software calculates midpoints as the dollar amount at the point where the pay policy line crosses the center of each grade. In **Exhibit 22**, the midpoints are drawn in the grades on the left. If you choose a policy line above or below the regression line, the midpoint will automatically adjust. *Midpoint Progression* is the average percent differential between salary midpoints in adjacent grades/ranges. **Exhibit 24** provides survey data on typical midpoint progression percentages used by organizations as a function of the type of pay structure they use. Most organizations use market-based structures with midpoint progressions that average around 16 %. Also shown is the number of salary grades/ranges that would be needed using different midpoint progressions (using a case where midpoints go from a minimum of 30,000 to a maximum of 200,000). One would need 14 grades/ranges in this case.

Minimums and Maximum

Range minimums and maximums (and midpoints) represent financial control points. Every job in a grade should be paid at least as much as the range minimum for that grade. No job in a grade should be paid more than the range maximum. Pay ranges also offer flexibility to adjust pay based on performance. Two people doing the same job can receive different pay rates and still be within the pay range for their job. Larger ranges are used when there is considerable room for individual differences in performance or experience.

Exhibit 24 Grade Midpoint Progression Practices and Number of Grades Needed (using example of low and high midpoints of 30k and 200k, respectively)

Example:

Lowest Salary Midpoint = 30,000
Highest Salary Midpoint = 200,000

Pay Structure Type	Midpoint Progression (median)	Grades Needed
Traditional (N = 139)	10%	21
Market-based (N = 443)	16%	14
Broadband (N = 66)	25%	10

Source: Midpoint Progression percentages computed using data reported in Table 3, "Salary Structure Policies and Practices," World at Work (and Deloitte Consulting LLP), October 2012. N is the number of organization respondents.

Midpoint Progression = percentage differential between adjacent grade midpoints.

Grades Needed = [natural log(Highest Salary Midpoint/Lowest Salary Midpoint)] ÷ [natural log(1 + Midpoint Progression)] + 1
[Hint: In Excel, use the ln function for natural log.]

Bands and Zones

Bands are often used to support more flexible organization designs. Some people think of them as "fat" grades. See the figure on the right of **Exhibit 22**. Bands reflect the natural breaks or shifts in the level of work. For example, in FastCat engineering work, it is feasible to construct three bands — Chief Engineer, Lead Engineer, and Associate Engineer — and slot the existing jobs into these three. Even a single band could be used (e.g., one BIG engineering job). Marketing work could be arranged in a similar manner, among three (or more/ fewer) bands. What approach fits best with what you know about FastCat? Which approach will help FastCat achieve its pay objectives?

Zones: Pay Rates for Jobs within Bands

If you use three bands for all the professional level work in FastCat, you will wind up with very different types and levels of work (e.g., engineers and marketers) in the same band. Conventional practice is to price professional work based on its market rate: engineering jobs in the Associate band are paid engineering market rates; marketers in the Associate band are paid a different market rate. Two zones, engineering and marketing, are established in the band. What are the tradeoffs FastCat will make if it uses banding? What will it gain?

One approach to decide size of zones is to return to the 75th percentile and 25th percentiles metrics in the software. These measures give you the boundaries of a zone that contains 50 percent of the pay rates in the market for a job or job family. The software requires at least one zone per band.

Exhibit 25 Band with Three Zones

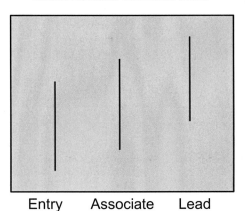

Entry   Associate   Lead

Exhibit 25 shows a band with Entry, Associate, and Lead zones. These zones could refer to either engineering or marketing work.

Which Policy for Which Grade/Band?

If you specified pay policy lines, you can apply your policy separately to each grade. A policy line has the effect of moving the midpoint and range up or down. Why bother? You may need to adjust to special situations in the market and/or to be consistent with the objectives you have set for external competitiveness. For example, if your objective was to lead the market for certain jobs, a policy line that is higher than the market line can apply to pay grades that contain those jobs. Or, if the slope of your regression line results in rates for entry-level jobs that you judge to be too low, you can set a higher policy line for these jobs.

Overlap

One way to judge how well your grades/ranges and bands/zones will work in actual practice is to examine the overlap between the maximum salary in a lower job grade and the minimum salary in successively higher grades. Trace the movement of a person over time and through several possible promotions to be sure your grades or bands support this movement.

Check the extremes of your overlap. Does the top paid person in grade 5, for example, deserve more than the "raw rookie" in grade 7 does (or whatever grade is the highest overlapping grade)? If the answer is yes, then the overlap may be acceptable. What difference does the degree of overlap make? Is the degree of overlap consistent with your compensation objectives?

The software gives you the ability to try a lot of different alternatives. Take advantage of the information you will get by modeling a number of different options. Then, recommend what you think is in FastCat's best interests and tell why. Keep in mind that the regression line is merely a statistic: a summary of the rates paid by competitors. It does not FORCE you to do anything. Be sure, oh please be sure, to use your analysis to support your recommendations. Use the roadmap at the beginning of this chapter as a guide to be sure you have covered the major issues.

STEP 5: EVALUATE YOUR DECISIONS

Based on your work on Phase I and your instructor's feedback, you should now have a fairly good sense of what to include in the report that you hand in for feedback and grading. Explain the process you went through to address each of the Phase II issues and justify your recommendations.

1. Your Strategy

Update the strategy. You began with Setting Objectives and a strategy for Internal Alignment. Then you specified a strategy for External Competitiveness. Are all these parts consistent with each other? Will they act in concert?

2. A Description of Your Analysis

What companies did you look at, and why? What jobs did you match? Why? What forms of pay did you analyze and what compensation metric did you use? Based on your analysis, what did you conclude about FastCat's competitors' pay practices?

How did you judge the results of your analysis? What did the statistics tell you? What policy line did you set, for which jobs/grades/bands, and why? How will this help FastCat?

At the Computer....

Reminder: For best results, proceed through the menu of Phase II tasks *in order* the first time you perform them. Do *not* skip ahead.

Click on either "Grades & Ranges" or "Bands & Zones".

GRADES & RANGES
In the top part of the form, choose from the pull-down list the number of grades you plan to include.
Grades will divide your structure along the x axis (JE points; skill/competency values).

Then design your grades.

* Step 1: For Grade 1, enter the lower and upper JE point for each grade. (For the rest of the grades, lower JE points is set automatically.)
* Step 2: Enter the size of the range (a percentage) for each grade. Ranges create a vertical area in each grade that accommodates paying different people doing the same job different pay rates.
* Step 3: Choose whether you wish to use the market line (the regression line), policy line 1, or policy line 2 as the midpoint for each grade.

If you do not wish to use ranges, you can create *flat rates* by omitting Step 2.

BANDS & ZONES
Directions are the same as for Grades and Ranges, with the following addition.
After you have designed Band I, move to the right side of the form and choose from the pull-down list the number of zones in Band 1. (You must have at least one zone per band.) Then set the JE points where you want the graph to draw that zone in that band. For example, if zone 1 goes from JE points 1 to 15, your band numbers for this zone must be between 1 and 15. Enter *in dollars* the zone minimums and maximums.

If you design all your bands before zones, return to the correct zones form by clicking in the corresponding band's data on the left side of the form.

Spend some time with the related **REPORTS: GRADES (or BANDS & ZONES) DATA**, and **GRADE (or BANDS & ZONES) GRAPH**. You will want to return to the graph many times as you try out different designs. Be sure to use the REGRESSION command after all your changes.

---

3. A Picture of Your Pay Structure(s)

How did you use the results of your analysis to help integrate FastCat's internal structure with the external market structure?

The end result of this phase is your recommended pay structure. <u>Include an exhibit</u> that details the pay structure, including the jobs in each grade or zone and the pay range for each grade, or zone or band. If you have a person-based plan, be sure to include the rates for each skill or competency level and the level that each of Fast-Cat's *current* jobs would fit into as part of your report. For example:

Current Job	Skill Level	Pay Rate
Technician	A	$34,300

Caution	*Do not simply attach computer printouts and expect your boss (or your instructor) to figure them out. Discuss the charts in your report – why you included them, what a reader should take away from them, how they support your recommendations.*

4. Rationale

Be sure to evaluate your results to be sure they are consistent with FastCat's values, business strategy, and compensation objectives. How are your decisions consistent with the company's strategy? How will they help the company in its new direction? If we seem fanatical about this, it's because these are always issues that interest senior management. Compensation is a major cost in most companies, and good managers always try to show how policies and pay decisions are linked to strategic objectives and not just costs.

Begin with an executive summary, and be prepared to present your results orally to your sympathetic but increasingly knowledgeable colleagues in your compensation class.

APPENDIX A: JOBS INCLUDED IN THE SURVEY

OFFICE SUPPORT 1

Entry level job. Performs a variety of clerical and other routine duties such as furnishing clerical supplies from stock, delivering verbal and written messages, sealing and stamping envelopes, running errands, collecting and distributing mail, answering telephones, and operating simple office machines such as copiers, postage meters, fax machines. Familiar with simple word processing and e-mail. Simple data entry. Works under close supervision.

OFFICE SUPPORT 2

Performs a variety of clerical and other routine duties. Working knowledge of word processing, spreadsheet software, and Powerpoint software. Accurate data entry into existing Access or Excel files. Can create PowerPoint presentations using templates. Familiar with Internet searching techniques. Answers telephones, provides routine information. Typical minimum requirement is one year of general office experience. Keeps supervisor informed of work progress.

OFFICE SUPPORT 3

Performs more advanced word processing, data entry, and spreadsheet tasks. May devise spreadsheet routines and develop standard reports; ensures the accuracy of data. Prepares PowerPoint presentations, charts, and graphs. Typical requirements are two to four years' experience.

OFFICE SUPPORT 4

Provides administrative support for project teams or managers at the level of department head. Sets up and maintains records, schedules appointments and meetings. Handles phone calls and email, draft responses on routine matters. If assigned to a project team, ensures all team members receive all communications. Prioritizes those communications that require managerial or team input. Handles sensitive and confidential information. Typical minimum requirements are four to six years' experience.

OFFICE SUPPORT 5

Provides administrative support for major executive. Sets up and maintains records, organizes and maintains daily schedule including appointments and meetings. Handles all communications, responds to routine matters. Prioritizes those communications that require executive input. Responsible for preparing executive presentations; may delegate tasks to lower-level support personnel. Position requires substantial discretion. Handles sensitive and confidential information. Typical minimum requirements are six to eight years experience.

OFFICE SUPPORT 6

Responsible for the smooth and efficient functioning of entire administrative support services group. Responsible for hiring and training support services personnel. Responsible for workflow in entire administrative support group. Typical minimum requirements are associates' degree and eight to ten years experience with demonstrated leadership experience.

MARKETER 1

Assists in providing support for one or a few products and generating presentations to incorporate marketing messages. Works under general direction dealing with less complex issues and products. Typical requirements are a Bachelor's degree or equivalent and up to two years of experience.

MARKETER 2

Assists in providing direction for one or a few products. Interacts with product management and customers to provide input at review meetings. Generates presentations to incorporate marketing messages. Typical requirements are a Bachelor's degree and two to four years of experience or a Master's degree and up to two years of experience.

MARKETER 3

Assists in providing direction for one or a few products. Interacts with product management and customers to provide input at review meetings. Provides support through demo instruction and tool development, functional demonstrations, and telephone consultation. Typical requirements are a Bachelor's degree and four to six years of experience or a Master's degree and two to four years of experience.

MARKETER 4

Coordinates overall strategy for a number of products or a product line. Interacts with product management and customers to provide input at review meetings. Maintains expertise of products through training and research. Helps develop product specifications and requirements. Typical requirements are a Bachelor's degree and six or more years of experience or a Master's degree and four to six years of experience.

MARKETER 5

Develops overall strategy for marketing a product line or product set. Maintains expertise of products through training and research. Key resource in interacting with product management and marketing groups. Develops product specifications and requirements. Typical requirements are a Bachelor's degree and ten or more years of experience or a Master's degree and six or more years of experience.

MARKETING MANAGER 1

Oversees the development of product specifications and requirements for a product line or a product set. Key resource in interacting with product management and marketing groups. Provides presentations to senior customer management. Typically manages up to 10 employees performing similar tasks. First level of management with human resource responsibilities.

MARKETING MANAGER 2

Defines company's strategy for multiple product lines. Manages the development of product specification and requirement strategies. Provides presentations to senior customer management. Typically manages 10 to 25 employees, including first level managers. (May be from multiple disciplines.)

MARKETING MANAGER 3

Creates, establishes, and manages the strategy for a significant portion of the company's product offering. Focuses on key products or next generation products and manages overall product marketing strategy. Typically manages over 25 employees from multiple disciplines.

TECHNICIAN 1

Under close supervision, assists in routine destructive testing procedures on software routines or systems. Entry level. Assumes no previous experience.

TECHICIAN 2

Using standard testing procedures and tools and under supervision, evaluates new or unique software routines to ensure its validity and accuracy. Thoroughly documents procedures and results. Typical minimum requirements are up to two years experience with computers.

TECHNICIAN 3

Using standard testing procedures and tools, evaluates new or unique software to ensure its validity and accuracy. May be responsible for ensuring internal consistency of complete software program. May also devise unique tests. Thoroughly documents procedures used and results. Typical minimum requirements are an associate's degree and two to four year's experience.

TECHNICIAN 4

Using standard and nonstandard testing procedures and tools, evaluates new or unique software to ensure its validity and accuracy. Devises unique tests for new products, works closely with software engineers to ensure adequate testing. Thoroughly documents procedures and results. May supervise other technicians. Typical minimum requirements are an associate's degree and four to six year's experience.

TECHNICIAN 5

Oversees the testing and debugging of software or software routines. Responsible for validity and accuracy of all software. Ensures that testers thoroughly document their results, communicates results to software programmers. Suggests ways to improve accuracy and efficiency of software product. Trains and oversees other technicians. May do only complex testing of strategically important products. Typical minimum requirements are an associate's degree and six to eight year's experience.

ENGINEER 1

Participates in development, testing and documentation of software programs. Performs design and analysis tasks as a project team member. Typical minimum requirements are a Bachelor's degree in a scientific or technical field or the equivalent and up to two years of experience.

ENGINEER 2

Develops, tests, and documents software programs of a more difficult nature. Assists in the development of assignments and schedules. Typical minimum requirements are a Bachelor's degree in a scientific or technical field and two to four years of experience or a Master's degree and up to two years of experience.

ENGINEER 3

Develops project plans, functional specifications and schedules. Designs and performs analysis on complex programs and systems. Assists in determining product needs and enhancements. Typical minimum requirements are a Bachelor's degree in Engineering, Computer Science or a related technical field and four to six years of experience or a Master's degree and two to four years of experience.

ENGINEER 4

Acts as project engineer for complex programs in design, development and analysis. Proposes new ideas and products and guides their implementation. Provides technical direction in area of specialty on major products. Typical minimum requirements are a Bachelor's degree in engineering, Computer Science or a related technical field and six or more years of experience or a Master's degree and four to six years of experience.

ENGINEER 5

Provides technical direction and advice to management in long-range planning for new areas of technological research. Designs, researches and develops new systems while providing guidance to support staff. Typical minimum requirements are a Bachelor's degree in engineering, Computer Science or a related technical field and ten or more years of experience or a Master's degree and six years or more of experience.

ENGINEERING MANAGER 1

Supervises the design and development of software products or systems and related schedules and costs. Participates in developing management policies for software group. Typically manages up to 10 employees performing similar tasks. First level of management with human resource responsibilities.

ENGINEERING MANAGER 2

Establishes work environment for development or implementation of complete products and programs. Develops long range plans, schedules and cost objectives. Typically manages 10 to 25 employees, including first level managers. (May be from multiple disciplines.)

ENGINEERING MANAGER 3

Develops long range strategy for a product family including positioning, marketing and pricing. Manages engineering product group to ensure timely delivery of high-quality products. Typically manages over 25 employees from multiple disciplines.

APPENDIX B: COMPANIES INCLUDED IN THE SURVEY

Company	Industry	Size	Base/Total Comp	Ben/Base	LTI/Base	STI/Base	Company	Industry	Size	Base/Total Comp	Ben/Base	LTI/Base	STI/Base
1	software	large	75%	29%	0%	5%	31	manufact	med	72%	36%	0%	3%
2	software	large	55%	28%	41%	15%	32	financial	med	64%	30%	18%	9%
3	financial	med	48%	32%	55%	20%	33	software	med	65%	17%	26%	12%
4	software	med	76%	30%	0%	1%	34	semicdctr	small	77%	22%	7%	1%
5	software	med	68%	26%	18%	3%	35	hardware	small	79%	22%	2%	2%
6	hardware	med	59%	27%	38%	6%	36	manufact	med	63%	50%	0%	8%
7	hardware	large	77%	28%	2%	1%	37	semicdctr	small	69%	22%	23%	1%
8	hardware	large	68%	39%	1%	8%	38	software	med	82%	20%	0%	1%
9	semicdctr	large	58%	24%	30%	19%	39	software	med	62%	36%	18%	8%
10	software	med	75%	31%	1%	0%	40	software	small	67%	35%	9%	4%
11	manufact	med	69%	27%	15%	2%	41	software	med	43%	23%	104%	5%
12	software	large	76%	26%	4%	2%	42	manufact	small	79%	26%	0%	0%
13	hardware	med	77%	25%	4%	1%	43	hardware	med	73%	28%	4%	5%
14	software	med	67%	43%	0%	6%	44	financial	small	47%	28%	77%	9%
15	software	large	64%	34%	5%	16%	45	software	small	75%	19%	12%	2%
16	semicdctr	med	79%	19%	2%	5%	46	software	small	73%	23%	11%	4%
17	financial	small	72%	25%	0%	14%	47	software	med	69%	30%	6%	8%
18	manufact	large	70%	42%	0%	0%	48	hardware	small	72%	28%	6%	6%
19	software	large	47%	37%	68%	8%	49	semicdctr	small	76%	26%	3%	2%
20	hardware	small	78%	25%	0%	4%	50	financial	small	69%	29%	10%	6%
21	financial	small	73%	26%	9%	2%	51	software	small	41%	22%	119%	3%
22	semicdctr	med	72%	27%	11%	2%	52	software	med	65%	26%	18%	9%
23	software	small	72%	18%	19%	2%	53	software	small	52%	19%	69%	4%
24	manufact	med	76%	32%	0%	0%	54	software	small	68%	24%	22%	0%
25	software	med	73%	25%	8%	3%	55	software	small	48%	24%	76%	7%
26	software	large	67%	32%	8%	8%	56	software	large	80%	25%	0%	0%
27	manufact	large	75%	27%	0%	8%	57	software	large	76%	28%	1%	3%
28	semicdctr	small	75%	22%	9%	2%	58	hardware	large	75%	28%	1%	4%
29	hardware	large	54%	28%	57%	1%	59	software	large	76%	28%	1%	3%
30	financial	small	70%	23%	12%	7%	60	software	med	76%	22%	5%	5%

base = base salary, STI = short term incentive, LTI = long term incentive, Total Comp = Total Compensation
hardware = computer hardware, software = computer software, manufact = manufacturing, semicdctr = semiconductor,
financial = financial services

PHASE III
PERFORMANCE
and
MANAGEMENT

In Phase III, you will use the compensation system you designed in Phases I and II to pay individual employees, develop plans that reward performance (both employees' and FastCat's), add benefits to the mix, and evaluate the results of your decisions. You will also propose a strategy for managing your system at FastCat.

Specially written software will help organize your Phase III decisions. Software directions are found near the pages on which a decision is discussed.

A road map for Phase III follows on the next page.

PHASE III (Performance and Management) STEPS

Step 1: Recommend Strategy for Performance-Based Pay
What performance-based pay strategies are available?
What performance-based pay strategy will best help
FastCat achieve its objectives?

Step 2: Assess Current Salaries
(Block One in the software)
Enter Phase II data and salary data on individual employees
Are current employee salaries consistent with FastCat's objectives?
Green circle rates? Red circle rates?
Any recommended salary adjustments?

Step 3: Design Merit Pay Plan
(Block Two in the software)
Objectives and rationale?
Cost and eligibility?
What will the distribution of performance ratings be?
How strongly do you recommend differentiating pay based on performance?
Threshold and cap?

Step 4: Design Bonus Plan (using Balanced Scorecard)
(Block Three in the software)
Objectives and rationale?
Criteria: Performance measures to be used in allocating bonuses?
Threshold and cap?

Step 5: Consider Any Other Performance-Based Pay Plans
Recommending other performance-based pay plans?
Objectives and rationale?

Step 6: Benefits
(Block Four in the software)
How is benefits strategy included in FastCat's compensation strategy?
What competitors are used for benchmarking?
What is the benefits to base pay ratio among selected competitors?
What benefits to base pay ratio is recommended for FastCat?

Step 7: How Will Your Recommendations Achieve Your Objectives?

Step 8: Recommend Strategy for Managing the System
How to monitor how well your strategy achieves FastCat objectives?
How to manage communication and participation?
How much to customize/offer employee choice?
How to evaluate?

And finally: <u>Write Your Report</u>

BACKGROUND

Ask Your
Instructor

Phase III addresses some final issues in FastCat's compensation system. Chapters 9, 10, and 11 of the *Compensation* textbook provide background on recognizing performance with pay. Chapters 12 and 13 cover the benefits determination process. Chapter 17 addresses legal compliance. Chapter 18 covers budgets and management. The FastCat background information included in the Introduction will also help you design the balanced scorecard. You will also need your results from Phases I and II. *Your instructor will give you salary information for a group of FastCat employees.* Use this information and the Phase III software to design your plans.

STEP 1: RECOMMEND STRATEGY FOR RECOGNIZING PERFORMANCE

In **Exhibit 26**, performance-based pay plans are compared on a number of dimensions. (See also Chapter 9 of *Compensation*.) The decisions called out in the first column provide a guide for designing and comparing plans. Use the information to decide what types of plans are appropriate in light of the work done at FastCat, its business strategy, your emerging compensation strategy, and your compensation objectives.

How will basing part of employees' pay on performance help FastCat compete? Specify FastCat's strategy for recognizing performance. Look in the Introduction and in the textbook for actual company statements about a pay-for-performance strategy. What do you hope to accomplish at FastCat with performance-based pay? Will your plan be based on individual performance, company performance, or both? What are its likely incentive and sorting effects? (See Chapters 1 and 9 of *Compensation*.)

STEP 2: ASSESS CURRENT SALARIES

Your instructor will give you current salaries for a group of FastCat employees. Keep in mind that you are not dealing with a statistical sample of employees; therefore changes in costs for this group will provide a precise estimate of the cost implications for FastCat overall, but they will provide some idea. The data on individual employees can be used to assess how performance, job tenure, and demographics affect (current) salaries. Be sure to address any concerns such data raise. Although most employees will probably fit into your system, some salaries may need immediate attention because they are below the minimum or above the maximum of the grade.

Green circle

Some salaries may be *below* the pay structure you built in Phases I and II. How should FastCat deal with this situation? First, check to be sure the job is properly evaluated and priced in the market (i.e., review your work in Phases I and II). Then lay out your options for handling these employees. Should you boost their salaries? Cut the salaries of people around them? Do nothing?

What are the tradeoffs (for example, labor costs, and fairness) of each option? How do you think the affected individual will react to your recommendation? How about that individual's coworkers? What reactions do you expect from the founders (who are the owners) of FastCat? There may be no recommendation that satisfies everyone. So be sure to state in your report how you will minimize the risks of what you recommend.

Red Circle

Some of the salaries may already be set too high for your pay structure. How will you deal with these situations? Again, check your work in Phases I and II, then lay out your options. In addition to adjusting the base wage, you can also move an employee into another job with a higher pay range. Does the person's performance level warrant a promotion?

DIRECTIONS FOR USING THE PHASE III SOFTWARE

The Phase III software has 4 blocks. Block one Adjusts employees into your system, Block Two is Merit Pay, Block Three is Bonus, Block Four is Benefits & Results. Have the following information handy before you start:

1. JE points (Phase I) for FastCat jobs
2. Information on your pay grades/bands and ranges and zones (Phase II)
3. Present pay rates for 25 FastCat employees (provided by instructor)

Reminder: For best results, proceed through the menu of Phase II tasks *in order* the first time you perform them. Do *not* skip ahead.

BLOCK ONE: INITIAL ADJUSTMENTS

Did you use grades and ranges in Phase II, or bands and zones? Click which one at the top of Block One.

Enter Your Phase II Pay Structure Data

1. Enter the job evaluation (JE) points for each grade or zone and the dollar minimums and maximums for each range or band.
   If you used bands, be sure to complete the right half of the screen, too.
2. Click on *View Graph* in upper right corner to be sure the graph looks the same as your results in Phase II.

Enter Initial Base (salaries provided by your instructor) for the sample of 25 FastCat Employees

Click on *View Graph* to see where employees fall in your grades or bands. This information will help you decide if you need to make any initial adjustments to base pay before you go on to the other parts of Phase III. The software offers several ways to assess present salaries. Look at the bar graph and the scatter graph to see all 25 employees at once. Look at the Employee Transactions page for each employee. If you decide to make any adjustments, do so on the *Employee Transactions* pages (one page for each employee).

Employee Transactions

The four parts of the Employee Transactions pages correspond to the four blocks of the software. Additional parts appear later in the program.

Initial Adjustments Part of the Employee Transactions Page

1. Move an employee into a new job by entering the grade/band number and JE points for the new job the employee will be going into. *(Do NOT do this in the case of a red circle or green circle rate.)* Type in the new job title in the space provided. Or, enter a new amount in the Adjusted Base line. Look at the background information on the employee (see **Appendix A** at the end of Phase III) to help you decide what action to take.
2. Pay attention to what effect your decisions have on each employee's compa-ratio
3. Use either the Record locator arrows at the bottom of the page or the link at the top right to move to another Employee Transactions page.
4. Use the *Pay Mix, Scatter,* and *Summary* links to see the results of your decisions.

*Remember that these are one-time changes to adjust the employees into your new system, done **before** you design any performance-based plans.*

SEPARATE STRUCTURES?

You will need to go through the Phase III software separately for each job structure. Then combine your results. Be sure all 14 jobs and 25 employees are included in your combined results.

NO JE POINTS?

If your structure does not have JE points, rank order the jobs in that structure with 1 being the lowest-ranking job. Then number the corresponding bands and zones. Enter these numbers. See the example:

Employee #	Job Title	Rank I give this job	Points	Band	Zone
10	Sr Qual Assurance Tech	3	3	2	2
11	Sr Qual Assurance Tech	3	3	2	2
12	Qual Analyst A	2	2	2	1
13	Qual Analyst A	2	2	2	1
14	Technician	1	1	1	1
15	Technician	1	1	1	1

Your graphs will look better if you put some width in your X axis by using more than one point per band. Otherwise all your bands and zones will pile up on top of each other.

STEP 3: DESIGN MERIT PAY PLAN

Organize your work on Issue Three around the dimensions in **Exhibit 26**. Chapters 9 - 11 in the *Compensation* textbook will also be useful.

Objectives and Rationale: What message does merit pay send to employees? How will merit pay be useful to managers and employees? Recall from the *Cases* Introduction that only 58% of employees said they understand how their pay is determined and only 45% said good performance is rewarded. Do they understand how their merit pay is determined? Does it matter? If it matters, how might FastCat increase their understanding? Does FastCat need to change how it pays?

Eligibility: Will all employees be part of the plan, or only those whose jobs allow for variability in performance? What will you recommend for those not covered by your merit plan?

Cost: Because merit increases add into base pay, labor costs are increased permanently. The size of that increase depends on the merit budget. Also, if larger merit increases go to employees having higher performance ratings, the distribution of ratings will also affect merit budget cost.

Performance Rating Distribution: FastCat has a performance appraisal/merit system that rates employee on a 5-point scale. Here is the distribution of FastCat ratings for the current year.

Rating	Rating Anchor	% employees receiving
1	Far exceeded requirements	25%
2	Exceeded requirements	55%
3	Met requirements	14%
4	Met some requirements	6%
5	Did not meet requirements	0%

Exhibit 26 Criteria for Comparing Performance-Based Pay Plans

DECISION	MERIT	GAINSHARING	PROFIT SHARING
Objectives, Philosophy	Signals meritocracy Individual contributions matter Long-term commitment Control costs	Signals performance philosophy Team contributions matter Short term Control costs	Signals performance philosophy Total unit membership matters Short term Control costs
Eligibility	All employees	Team members	Professionals & managers most common
Cost Effects	Increases fixed costs	Variable	Variable
Performance Measures	Performance appraisal ratings	Team level measures (costs, quality, quantity)	Unit-level financials (ROA, ROI, ROC)
Threshold	Minimum performance rating	Minimum cost, quality, quantity	Minimum financial return required
Cap	Merit budget	Ceiling on payouts	Ceiling on payouts
Schedule: Size, Timing	Merit grid	By performance achieved	By performance achieved
Form of Pay	Cash spread over budget cycle	Cash lump	Cash lump
Manage Plan & Changes	Communication	Communication, participation	Communication, participation

FastCat uses a grid that combines performance ratings with the distribution of employees in the pay range for their job. Last year the distribution of employees across quartiles, Q1 through Q4 (which are based on compa-ratios), in their pay ranges was as follows:

Q4	30%
Q3	22%
Q2	21%
Q1	27%

Combining these two distributions creates a merit increase grid that distributes all FastCat employees among the 20 cells in the grid according to each employee's performance rating and quartile (position in the pay range and/or compa-ratio) for their job (**Exhibit 27**). Once employees are slotted into cells in the grid, you can decide what size merit increase to give to employees in each cell. Several exhibits in Chapter 11 of the *Compensation* textbook show the logic behind merit increase grids. Consider modeling other possible distributions. For example, what would be the effect of a forced distribution?

Thresholds

Should all employees receive a merit increase? What about those whose performance falls below a certain level? For example, 8 percent of FastCat employees met only some of their job requirements. Should they receive a merit increase?

Ask Your Instructor

Cap

The cap is the budget set by management. Generally, companies set a merit budget to match the percentage that the market is moving, i.e., your update percentage in Phase II. *Ask your instructor if you should set the cap yourself or if one will be given to you?*

Exhibit 27
Merit Increase Grid

Performance Ratings

Compa-Ratio/ Quartile

1   2   3   4   5

Performance is weak, plus they are already paid high in their range

Center of Grid

Performance is great here plus room to move up in pay range

Decide what the cell entries should be in Exhibit 27. Should employees be kept whole with respect to increases in their labor market? If your answer is yes, one way might be to insure that employees with satisfactory performance

At the Computer...

BLOCK TWO: MERIT PAY
Distribute by Quartile and Performance

Enter the merit and performance distributions and your merit increase budget cap. As you allocate increases in the cells of the grid (using the "**Design Merit Grid**" button), a running total of the percentage allocated appears at the bottom of the screen. This tells you when you hit your cap.

View Employee Distribution in Grid.

To see which employees fall in each cell in the grid, jump from this screen to a particular **Employee Transaction** sheet to see the size of the merit increase or to exclude a particular employee from the merit pay plan (by selecting No). If you do not wish to vary pay with individual performance, enter the same percent in each cell.

and in the middle of their range receive an increase equal to your merit budget. Put this amount in the cells near the center of the grid.

How much of a percentage pay difference should result from each increment in performance? Are these differences great enough to motivate performance? Will they support your strategy? Your answer will guide your entries for cells to the left of the center.

Should workers higher in the pay range receive lower increases for the same level of performance?

Some argue that a "yes" implies that increments in performance are smaller over time. Others argue that even though the percent may be smaller, the dollar amounts may still be larger, since they are calculated on a larger base. Your answers will guide your choice of % increases to use in the merit increase grid.

Should employees whose performance is below average receive any increase at all? Should it depend on where the employee is (quartile, compa-ratio) in the pay grade? For example, what if an employee has worked at FastCat only a short time? A long time?

One can think in terms of where an employee's base pay should be relative to the market if s/he consistently performs at a particular level. A consistently average performer ("met expectations") should be paid at "market" (i.e., at the midpoint), whereas an employee with consistently above average ("exceeds expectations") performance should be paid above the midpoint. However, if merit increases were to be given without any attention to current position in range, the risk is that even for a high performer, the base pay would eventually increase far beyond the employee's value in the market for doing that job.

Keep in mind that the numbers you put in the cells in the grid translate strategy into practice. Are your allocations consistent with your strategy?

STEP 4: DESIGN BONUS PLAN (USING BALANCED SCORECARD)

A balanced scorecard can help you pay FastCat employees based on company performance rather than individual performance. FastCat does not presently have such a plan, but you have been asked to design one using a balanced scorecard. Once again, **Exhibit 26** provides a launching pad for your design decisions. Be sure to read about balanced scorecard in Chapter 10 of the *Compensation* textbook, too.

Objectives/Rationale: Does a bonus plan make sense for FastCat? Review the survey data in Phase II. All but a handful of the companies paid bonuses (short-term incentives). How many of these are FastCat competitors? How will bonuses fit FastCat's business objectives? What message does a bonus plan send to employees? How will a balanced scorecard help achieve objectives? Is a bonus plan consistent with your external competitive strategy?

Exhibit 28 Possible Metrics for Balanced Scorecard

Revenue

Growth

Labor Costs

Innovation

Customers see FastCat representatives as responsive and knowledgeable

Customers value FastCat solutions

Employees take pride in working for FastCat

Employees have the tools and support to do their jobs

Employees understand how to make teams successful

The notion behind a balanced scorecard is that it will create a clear, measurable link between business strategy and performance. A scorecard can facilitate communication. Does yours?

Eligibility: Will all FastCat employees be eligible for a bonus? Or will you give a bonus only to those considered strategically important? Will all eligible employees get equal shares of the bonus? Or will the payout vary with the pay structure, i.e., jobs at the top of the structure get larger payouts? These decisions are all related to the strategy for your plan. What do FastCat competitors do?

Cost Effects: By design, bonuses will vary with company performance and typically do not permanently increase individual base pay.

Criteria: Performance Measures to be Used: Exhibit 28 lists some possible measures of FastCat performance. These are included in the software.

(1) Decide which of these metrics to include in your plan (and tell why in your report).
(2) Decide how much weight to give each metric (and why).
(3) Decide how well FastCat is doing on each metric. The software will then calculate the size of the bonus pool, based on your decisions.

Be sure to review the FastCat history in the Introduction part of the casebook to answer these questions before you use the software. State the rationale for the metrics you include in your bonus plan. Recognize limitations of these measures and how you will minimize them. Propose other metrics that would have provided better information, if you like.

Thresholds: The threshold establishes the performance below which you do not want the plan to pay any increases. If the weighted score you give FastCat on the metrics of your choosing is below 3, there will be no bonus. However, any score of 3 or over generates a bonus to be distributed to those employees you decided were eligible.

Caps: In previous years, the cap has been 15% of base pay, paid out with a score of 5 (maximum). These limits were set by FastCat financial planners. You may wish to recommend different thresholds and caps for next year in your report. Be sure to include an evaluation of the current plan in your report.

STEP 5: CONSIDER ANY OTHER PERFORMANCE-BASED PAY PLANS

If you decide to propose some other performance pay plan for FastCat (i.e., phantom stock options, team-based pay, tickets to sporting events, trips to resort locations [Minnesota gets mighty cold in January]), include a description of your plan in your report. Using the criteria in **Exhibit 26**, provide the rationale for your plan, eligibility, etc. What would be the advantages and disadvantages of your plan?

STEP 6: BENEFITS

Part 4 of the *Compensation* textbook begins by suggesting that digging a hole in the ground and throwing money into it may be as effective a use of money as paying benefits. Of course this is an exaggeration; we know that benefits matter to employees. We also know they are very costly. So they impact FastCat labor costs and productivity metrics such as Revenues/Labor Costs (discussed in the FastCat introduction). But beyond knowing that they are costly and very important to employees, we know little else about how benefits affect the objectives of any pay system. Unlike performance-based pay plans, there is little evidence to understand benefits' effects on individuals and employers. Because benefits are so costly, they must be included in the design of your compensation system.

Studying how well benefits are managed at FastCat will be an excellent assignment for your replacement next year. Your assignment will be simply to make a budget prediction for benefits costs. This will help you better understand the cost implications of your compensation decisions to date.

Making this prediction involves the following steps:

A. Include Benefits in FastCat's Compensation Strategy

B. Select Relevant Competitors

C. Analyze Competitors' Benefits to Base Pay Ratios

D. Recommend a Benefits Ratio for FastCat

A. Include Benefits in FastCat's Compensation Strategy

In your Report for Phase II did you recommend that FastCat meet, lead or lag its competitors' compensation? Will you recommend extending that same strategy to benefits at FastCat? A quick review of the discussion of alternative compensation strategies in Chapter 7 of the *Compensation* textbook may be useful. The illustration in **Exhibit 29** shows alternatives for FastCat's competitive position with respect to base pay (lead, meet or lag: your decision in Phase II) and to benefits (your decision here). The exhibit also shows what we know about the results of a benefits strategy. Costs are certainly affected; but beyond that, we are less certain.

Exhibit 29 Eternal Competitive Strategy Alternatives

BASE PAY +	BENEFITS	RESULTS		
		Contain Costs	Productivity	Attract/Retain /Motivate
Lead	Lead Meet Lag	- - - + - +	?	?
Meet	Lead Meet Lag	+ - + + + +	?	?
Lag	Lead Meet Lag	+ - + + + +	?	?

Be sure to discuss how you think your recommendation (e.g. opting to lead your competition in both base pay and in benefits or to lead in base pay but meet competition with benefits) will affect your costs as well as people's behaviors. What do you think will be the effect on the objectives you recommended for your pay system (cost containment, productivity, innovate, attract, retain, motivate,…)? Much of this decision process, as noted in the *Compensation* textbook, must rely on your judgment due to the lack of guidance from useful evidence.

B. Select and Compare to Relevant Competitors

The market survey of competitors in Phase II includes the ratio of benefits to base pay for the 60 companies in the survey. **Appendix B** of Phase II also shows this information.

The *Compensation* textbook reports that benefits are, on average, more than 40% of payroll in U.S. companies. By contrast, you will see that the highest benefits to base ratio in the survey used by FastCat is 33%. *(Multiply the ratios shown in the software by 100 to get the corresponding percentage.)* Why the difference? The 40% plus figure includes legally required benefits such as Workers Compensation, Social Security, and Unemployment Insurance. Because U.S. companies have no or limited discretion over these amounts, they often do not include them in surveys of competitors' practices. Also, we know that benefits tend to vary with company size, with larger companies offering more benefits, on average.

C. Calculate the Benefits to Base Ratio among Relevant Competitors

The benefits ratios in the Phase II companies range from .12 to .33. Which of these companies are relevant to FastCat's competitive position on benefits? Are these the same companies that you chose for your Phase II decisions? Why or why not? You may wish you had more detailed benefits information from FastCat competitors. However, this is the only benefits data collected in this survey. Perhaps in the future FastCat will participate in surveys which include more detailed descriptions of the types of benefit plans offered. You may wish to recommend such a survey in your report. If you do, be sure to explain how that additional information would improve your decisions. (It certainly would increase your administrative costs.)

Of the companies you selected as relevant comparisons, will you calculate an average benefits ratio? Or a median? Does it matter? You decide which is most useful, and do the calculation.

D. Recommend a Benefits Ratio for FastCat

Enter the ratio using the software. The ratio you select will directly impact FastCat's labor costs. Perhaps it will also impact employee behaviors and thus the success of FastCat. Be sure to discuss the potential impact in your write-up.

At the Computer...

BLOCK FOUR: BENEFITS & RESULTS

Benefits:
Enter the amount you wish to spend on benefits.

Employee Transactions:
1. View the **Summary Info and Costs** section for each employee.
2. Click on **Pie** to see how the pay form percentages vary among employees.

View FastCat Costs & Summary Data:
Use the summary measures to judge the effects of your decisions.

COMBINING RESULTS

For each structure, you will need to re-enter the same numbers for merit pay and bonus (unless you are proposing different merit increases for different structures).

When you are satisfied with your decisions for a structure, go to **View FastCat Costs and Summary Data**.

Note: If you have more than one structure, you will need to manually compute the total cost of overall compensation and each compensation component.

STEP 7: HOW WILL YOUR RECOMMENDATIONS ACHIEVE YOUR OBJECTIVES?

The final step using the Phase III software is to consider the effects of all your Phase III decisions on the individual employees and the financial impact of your decisions. In order to judge whether you achieved your objectives, begin by putting all your data together.

- Summarize your recommended pay increases for the employees. This is part of the Summary data in the Results section of the software (Block Four). Each employee may have up to three types of pay increases:
    - Adjustment into the pay structure;
    - Merit increases; and
    - Bonus.

Be sure to discuss the costs for each type of increase, total costs involved, and the rate of change in these costs. For each initial adjustment into the structure, justify your recommendation.

- Evaluate your decisions in light of your strategy for performance pay and your compensation strategy, including benefits and costs. The FastCat Summary data provides cost information. However, be sure to review the Summary information for each employee, too.
- Evaluate your results in light of your alignment strategy. Is the salary structure consistent with the job structure you proposed in Phase I? Are there any individuals or jobs to flag for further investigation?

- Evaluate your results in light of your competitiveness strategy. On a graph of your results from Phase II, plot the new salaries for the 25 employees. Where do they lie? Are they consistent with your strategy? For example, if you had wanted to lag the market with base pay, do you? If you wanted to lead the market with total compensation, do you?

The software contains a lot of summary information, but it's your job to interpret it for your boss and discuss your recommendations in the context of what you are trying to achieve. ***Do not simply attach computer print-outs and expect your instructor to figure them out. Discuss the charts in your report – why you included them, what a reader should take away from them, how they support your recommendations.***

STEP 8: RECOMMEND STRATEGY FOR MANAGING THE SYSTEM

The final part of your compensation strategy is managing the system. How will you see that your plan runs as intended? Are there any changes you want to make to your Phase I and II recommendations based on what you know now (and what your instructor told you in feedback on your work so far)? How will you ensure that employees understand your system? Propose a strategy for managing the system. The issues below will give you some ideas. Don't feel you need to answer all the questions posed. They are merely to remind you to address these topics.

Monitor How Well Your System Achieves FastCat's Objectives

How will you decide if your system is actually behaving the way you intend? How will others know? Develop some measures to assess your system's behavior, tell how these measures will work, and why they are needed.

One way to determine what indexes will be useful is to reconsider your recommendations in all three phases. Decide what measures will highlight whether the system is getting results you seek. The software includes information about costs. However, you likely had additional objectives for your compensation system beyond controlling costs. Was an objective to treat employees fairly? The chart in **Appendix A** summarizes data about past salary treatment of FastCat employees. Are there any patterns in this data that causes concern? Does FastCat appear to be treating employees fairly? How will you know if your plan is fair? What effects of the plan might you wish to evaluate, and how will you do it?

Communication/Participation

Here is where you get to discuss your communication and participation plan. As you recall from the introduction, employees tend to trust management to communicate honestly. But there is room for improvement, particularly about how pay is determined. What should employees be told about their pay and how it fits into the overall compensation system? How will you manage employee expectations?

Should the organization have a communications process which is relatively closed or open? Should it emphasize "marketing" the pay program like one would market other products to customers? How is compensation part of FastCat's "HR Brand"? What recourse will employees have if they are dissatisfied with either their pay or your system?

Employee Choice/Customization

How much choice will you offer employees in their benefits? How about among various forms of pay? What are the tradeoffs in offering choice?

Evaluation: Continuous Improvement

No plan will be perfect; conditions change. So design continuous improvement into your recommendations. You probably already have some ideas for changes. Here is the chance to vent all those frustrations about procedures at FastCat. Perhaps you feel that the job descriptions used in Phase I should be redone? Perhaps the survey used in Phase II is not up to your standards? Or, the performance appraisal system needs revamping? Perhaps you wish to collect data so you can put in a team-based gain-sharing plan? Or you may want to purchase (or develop) some enterprise software to help managers manage compensation. Are any of the issues identified by the balanced scorecard related to the management of your compensation system? Propose and prioritize projects to address these issues. Recognize that FastCat cannot afford to make all changes at once. Which proposals do you think will deliver the most bang for FastCat's bucks? Can FastCat afford your recommendations? If the founders fund your budget, these projects can be tackled next year.

If you recommend new projects, include a very brief description of each project, rationale for your recommendations, and estimated costs, including salaries for people to do them. To come up with cost estimates, you might consider the amount of time you spent on the entire FastCat project. Based on that, estimate the number of hours each of your proposed projects would take. Salaries may be based on the starting salaries graduates at your school receive. These figures can help you estimate salary costs. Any other costs would depend on what projects you recommend.

"STEP 9": CELEBRATE YOUR SUCCESS

Give yourself a pat on the back. When you have completed Phase III, you have designed a pay system. The techniques you have used and the issues you faced are familiar to managers throughout the world. Students throughout North America and even in Europe and Asia tell their instructors this course is a lot of work, but they have learned a lot. Some even use their cases in job interviews to demonstrate their experience.

Throughout this course, you handled a rich variety of problems. By comparing your decisions with those of your classmates, you have discovered the rich variety of solutions. Take these ideas with you to the workplace, where you will be able to help make pay systems more efficient, more fair, more productive. Playing with other people's money can be a lot of fun — and it pays well, too!

(Appendix A FastCat Employee Data on Next Page)

Appendix A
FastCat Employees

Ee#	Current Job Title	Performance (1=High, 5=Low)	Years in Job	Last Merit Increase	Gender	Minority Group Member
1	Administrative Aide	1	2	4	f	y
2	Administrative Leader	4	1	1	f	y
3	Clinical Liaison	1	4	5	f	n
4	Clinical Liaison	3	1	2	f	y
5	Graphic Designer	3	1	2	f	y
6	Graphic Designer	1	2	3	m	n
7	Marketing Services Rep	1	4	3	f	n
8	Marketing Services Rep	1	1	2	m	y
9	Programmer Analyst	3	3	2	m	n
10	Programmer Analyst	1	8	4	f	n
11	Project Leader	1	6	4	f	n
12	Project Support Assistant	1	3	3	m	y
13	Project Support Assistant	2	4	2	f	y
14	Quality Assurance Analyst	4	6	2	m	y
15	Quality Assurance Analyst	1	2	3	f	n
16	Senior Quality Assurance Technician	1	1	4	f	n
17	Senior Quality Assurance Technician	2	5	4	m	y
18	Software User Interface Architect	2	4	3	f	n
19	Software User Interface Architect	1	3	5	m	n
20	Training Assistant	2	8	4	f	n
21	Training Assistant	3	3	2	m	n
22	User Interface Designer	3	7	2	m	y
23	User Interface Designer	1	4	5	m	n
24	Visionary Champion	2	6	3	m	y
25	Visionary Champion	2	7	4	f	n